THE
SECRET
HISTORY
OF BALLS

THE SECRET HISTORY OF BALLS

The Stories Behind the Things We Love to Catch, Whack, Throw, Kick, Bounce, and Bat

JOSH CHETWYND

Illustrations by Emily Stackhouse

A PERIGEE BOOK

A PERIGEE BOOK
Published by the Penguin Group
Penguin Group (USA) Inc.
375 Hudson Street, New York, New York 10014, USA
Penguin Group (Canada), 90 Eglinton Avenue East, Suite 700, Toronto, Ontario M4P
2Y3, Canada (a division of Pearson Penguin Canada Inc.)
Penguin Books Ltd., 80 Strand, London WC2R 0RL, England
Penguin Group Ireland, 25 St. Stephen's Green, Dublin 2, Ireland
(a division of Penguin Books Ltd.)
Penguin Group (Australia), 250 Camberwell Road, Camberwell, Victoria 3124, Australia
(a division of Pearson Australia Group Pty. Ltd.)
Penguin Books India Pvt. Ltd., 11 Community Centre, Panchsheel Park,
New Delhi—110 017, India
Penguin Group (NZ), 67 Apollo Drive, Rosedale, Auckland 0632, New Zealand
(a division of Pearson New Zealand Ltd.)
Penguin Books (South Africa) (Pty.) Ltd., 24 Sturdee Avenue, Rosebank, Johannesburg
2196, South Africa
Penguin Books Ltd., Registered Offices: 80 Strand, London WC2R 0RL, England

While the author has made every effort to provide accurate telephone numbers and
Internet addresses at the time of publication, neither the publisher nor the author
assumes any responsibility for errors or for changes that occur after publication.
Further, the publisher does not have any control over and does not assume any
responsibility for author or third-party websites or their content.

First edition: May 2011

Library of Congress Cataloging-in-Publication Data

Chetwynd, Josh.
The secret history of balls : the stories behind the things we love to catch, whack,
throw, kick, bounce and bat / Josh Chetwynd ; Illustrations by Emily Stackhouse.
     p.   cm.
"A Perigee Book."
Includes bibliographical references.
   ISBN 978-0-399-53674-8 (pbk.)
   1. Balls (Sporting goods)—History.   2. Ball games—History.   3. Toys—History.
I. Title.
   GV749.B34C44 2011
   796.3—dc22   2010054221

PRINTED IN THE UNITED STATES OF AMERICA

10   9   8   7   6   5   4   3   2   1

Most Perigee books are available at special quantity discounts for bulk purchases for
sales promotions, premiums, fund-raising, or educational use. Special books, or book
excerpts, can also be created to fit specific needs. For details, write: Special Markets,
Penguin Group (USA) Inc., 375 Hudson Street, New York, New York 10014.

For Miller and Becca:
May you always have a ball

CONTENTS

Introduction   XI

Australian Rules football   1
Ba' (Shrovetide football, festival   4
    football, Cornish hurling ball)
Bandy ball   7
Baseball   10
Basketball   16
Beach ball   22
Bearing balls (ball bearings)   26
Billiard balls (snooker ball)   28
Bocce balls   34
Bowling ball   36
Cricket ball   40
Croquet balls   43
Exercise ball (Swiss ball)   46
Field hockey ball   49
Footbag (Hacky Sack)   52
Football   54
Gaelic football   60
Golf ball   62
Handball   67
Jai alai pelota   70

Ki   74

Koosh Ball   77

Lacrosse ball   79

Lawn bowling balls (bowls/woods)   82

Magic 8 Ball   87

Marbles   89

Mari   95

Medicine ball   98

Meditation balls   100

Nerf ball   103

Netball   107

Paintballs   108

Pallo   112

Pétanque boules   114

Pinball   118

Pink ball (Spaldeen, Pennsy Pinky)   121

Polo ball   125

Pushball (bladderball, cage ball)   128

Racquetball   131

Red playground ball   134
    (cherry ball, red utility ball)

Roulette ball   137

Rugby ball   141

Shot put   144

Sliotar   147

Soccer ball   151

Softball   155

Space Hopper   160
    (Hopper, Ride-a-Roo,
    Kangaroo Ball, Hoppity Hop)

Squash ball   164
Stress ball   167
SuperBall   170
Table tennis ball (Ping-Pong ball)   174
Takraw (Raga)   177
Team handball   180
Tennis ball   182
Tetherball   188
Ulama ball   191
Volleyball   193
Water polo ball   196
Wiffle Ball   198
Zorb Globe   201

Acknowledgments   207
Notes   209
Sources and Further Reading   217

INTRODUCTION

First things first: Before embarking on a history of balls, we need to know what we're talking about. Depending on the conversation, the word can mean courage, a part of the male anatomy, a place where Cinderella longs to go, or a thing pretty much every human has played with at one time or another. For the purpose of this book, we're looking at the latter (apologies to those who expected something a little saucier).

Even when we get that far, there are still questions. What exactly constitutes a ball? Does it have to be round? Does it have to bounce? Is a sphere the same as a prolate spheroid (the technical term for the shape of a football or a rugby ball)? These are questions that have vexed even the greatest of athletes. Once, after an Irish rugby star finished a big match, he ran into writer James Joyce at the local bar. The erudite author told the player, "Y'didn't play with a ball today, by definition balls are round; nor even with an oval, which demands a plane configuration; y'played with a prolate spheroid." Without skipping a beat, the player reportedly responded: "Jaysus, Jim, so that's what I bleddy scored with!"

With all due respect to Joyce, nowadays a ball means so much more than just a sphere. I've opted to cover just about every "rounded body" (definition courtesy of *Encyclopedia Britannica*'s 1911 edition) that gives us joy on the field, at stadiums and arenas, or in backyards and living rooms around the globe. It didn't matter whether it was a sphere, oval, or prolate spheroid; hollow, solid, full of air or liquid, or stuffed with twine; made of leather, metal, rubber, plastic, or polyurethane. I even included the Magic 8 Ball, because, quite honestly, it was too much fun to pass up. One final caveat: Focus remained on the balls still in play today (and their direct ancestors). So the long-gone sphere used in the ancient Greek sport *episkyros* (an old school kicking and throwing game) didn't make the cut.

With the ground rules out of the way, I should explain why I wanted to do a book on this topic (besides all the fun jokes friends brought up while I was putting it together). Quite simply, balls are the unsung heroes of sports. They are wacked, smacked, slapped, splattered, flicked, flung, dribbled, crushed, thrown, tossed, and kicked. Alas, despite their central role, balls usually only make headlines when something goes wrong: a tear, the application of an illegal foreign substance, or a dent from overuse. This fact seems a bit odd because if you watch nearly any major sporting event, you're likely following the ball, wondering where *it* will go next.

In a way, the modern plight of the ball is particularly surprising because it used to sit center stage. It was a religious artifact in many cultures, and in others it's been a fantastically polarizing element. On the one hand, you've had great leaders who gravitated to ball games. The roster of ballplayers is prestigious: Alexander the Great, Genghis Kahn, Augustus Caesar, Mary Queen of Scots, Henry VIII, Sir Francis Drake, and Abraham Lincoln, to name a few. But for every sphere supporter, there has been a leader who saw balls—and their games—as something subversive or degrading. Kings, potentates, and officials from Scotland to Spain and New York to New Zealand have shunned various ball games over the centuries. The typical reasons: The game encouraged gambling or took away from more important pursuits such as military preparation. Thomas Jefferson was a particular critic. He once wrote a nephew warning the young man to avoid ball sports because "[g]ames played with the ball . . . are too violent for the body and stamp no character on the mind." Famed British writer Jerome K. Jerome joked that if celestial beings looked down on earth and saw humans playing ball, they would be convinced that "the [b]all must be some malignant creature of fiendish power, the great enemy of the human race."

So what has consigned balls to supporting status? Maybe it has something to do with the industrial revolution and mechanization. Once balls could be mass-produced, the little idiosyncrasies that made them come to life seemed to disappear. When every ball is meant to play the same, no wonder people only notice when it's acting oddly. That said, this doesn't mean that balls don't have a personality. Like people, they are the product of generations of evolution. Elements that we take for granted—including dimples on a golf ball, laces on a football, or a tennis ball's fuzzy fur—are often a reflection of forgotten decisions and actions (some long ago and others more recent). These stories have included class warfare; star-crossed lovers, great minds, world-altering inventions, and matters of life and death.

This volume mines the history of sports and recreation to offer those tales through the origins and development of sixty balls (plus, if you read closely, information on a handful of other orbs). The book aims to be comprehensive but not exhaustive. The reason: Where there are people who want to have some fun, you'll always find some new or obscure ball popping up. My goal is that after taking a read, you'll agree with Pulitzer Prize–winning author Barbara Tuchman, who wrote: "In human activity, the invention of the ball may be said to rank with the invention of the wheel." Even if you don't, hopefully you won't look at a ball—any ball—the same way again.

Australian Rules football

If a soccer ball and a rugby ball were to have a love child, it would probably look like the oval-shaped, snubbed-nosed spheroid known as the *Australian Rules football*. There's a good reason for that: The birth of the Aussie Rules football was a result of a colonial tussle between early proponents of soccer and rugby.

In the mid-nineteenth century, Melbourne, Australia, was one of the world's most cosmopolitan cities. Beginning in 1851 with the Victorian gold rush, it became a hub for transport and a magnet for middle-class—and some wealthy—British fortune seekers. Along with working hard, these ex-pats also wanted to play. Most Anglo-Saxon newcomers to Australia had dabbled in Britain's emerging team sports of soccer—known as association football—and rugby. Nevertheless, the independent-minded settlers aimed to create their own code.

Deciding on the shape of the ball would indicate whether soccer supporters or rugby fans would have a greater influence on the new Australian game. The soccer ball appeared to be the initial front-runner as the sphere of choice. Some early rules—for example, requiring the ball only be picked up "on the hop"—seemed to support using an easy-bouncing round ball (the oblong rugby ball would skip unpredictably off the turf). Still, this issue was so unsettled that some contests began with an oval ball but ended with a round ball if the original orb burst.

Even after formal rules were established around 1860, different factions remained steadfastly in favor of one ball or the other. One of the sport's founders, Tom Wills, eventually gave rugby fans the advantage. A native Australian, Wills had attended the Rugby School in England and, predictably, was a supporter of the sport that carried his alma mater's name. Wills insisted on using the rugby ball every chance he got.

Beyond Wills's personal interest, some believe this conflict over the ball was actually a proxy for class warfare. Soccer-like codes were most popular at England's most elite public schools such as Eton and Harrow, while newer British institutions that taught the middle class—like Wills's Rugby School—played the rougher sport of rugby. In Melbourne, middle-class émigrés from England outnumbered the rich, and as a result, the rugby ball prevailed as the game ball in the 1870s.

Even though rugby's spheroid won the battle, concessions still had to be made for the soccer ball. After all, the round orb just made more sense when it came to some of the agreed-upon rules (for instance, bouncing the ball). T. W. Sherrin stepped into the void. A saddle maker, Sherrin set up shop in a Melbourne suburb and in his spare time enjoyed the Aussie Rules game. With his ties to the sport, Sherrin earned business repairing the rugby-style footballs. The sport was rough and the balls he fixed were often terribly tattered. He became an expert repairman, completely reconstructing many of the spheroids. Noticing the balls wore heaviest at the tips, Sherrin came up with a version featuring rounder points. His new option would not only solve the problem of wear but also make the ball easier to bounce and kick. His creation—mainly rugby, but part soccer—was the long-needed compromise between the ball options.

STATS AND FACTS

Dimensions: The ball is between 23.2 and 24.4 inches in diameter and generally weighs 16 to 17 ounces.

Aboriginal Roots: Some scholars claim that the sport was inspired at least in part by an Aboriginal game called *Marngrook*. A rugby-esque sport played with a ball made of opossum hide stuffed with charcoal or feathers, *Marngrook* was likely witnessed by founding father Tom Wills in his childhood. This assertion has been hotly contested by other writers.

Language: The Australian football has had numerous nicknames during its history, including *the pill*, *the nut*, *the tooty*, *the footy*, *the T.W.*, *the cherry*, *the agat*, *the Tommy*, and *the air conveyance*.

Ba' (Shrovetide football, festival football, Cornish hurling ball)

For the vast majority of people worldwide, the word *football* conjures up images of either soccer or the grid-iron (for those Down Under, they may also picture their unique Aussie Rules game). But in Ye Olde England it was a completely different kind of beast.

Centuries ago, teams of hundreds of men in Great Britain would square off in an anything-goes fiesta of clawing, kicking, pushing, and elbowing. Typically the objective was to get a ball—using hands, feet, or any body part—from the middle of town to a spot either at the top of the village or at the bottom. These events were often played on holidays with Shrove Tuesday (the day before the beginning of Lent) being the most popular. Although it was banned by various kings over the centuries because of its rowdy mob elements (does that surprise you?), this form of football, dubbed today as *festival* or *Shrovetide football*, continues to survive in pockets of the British Isles in annual local contests.

Despite the mass of humanity, the ball—typically dubbed the *ba'* in Scotland or simply the *ball* in England—is treated with serious respect. In one town, any smudged paint is touched up after the contest to leave the orb flawless for posterity. Financing its annual construction is usually a civic duty whereby members of the community ante up cash to manufacture the orb. In one hamlet, the parish clerk has been historically responsible for supplying the ball. Elsewhere, every local newlywed couple must provide a ball.

Design is painstakingly considered as well. In Scottish border towns, the ball, known as a *handba'*, tends to be small and durably constructed—though ribbons are added to give precocious young men a pickup technique. The player who pulls a ribbon off a ball can present it to a pretty young maiden he fancies in the audience. The stuffing is equally important. In the Scottish island town of Kirkwall, the soccer-ball-sized ba' takes four days to make and is stuffed tightly with cork dust to make sure it floats if one of the teams reaches its goal: a harbor at the bottom of the town. In Cornwall, located in the far southwest corner of England, the ball is the most intrinsically valuable. In the towns of St. Columb Major and St. Ives, it is fashioned from silver and bears such inspiring

Cornish mottos as "Town and Country do your best" and "Fair play is good play."

Anything tends to go when game time starts. In England's East Midlands, the ball employed in the town of Atherstone is the largest of all (think beach ball dimensions). As a result, when the game nears its climax, competitors will cut it open to make it easier to hold on to. As the national sport of soccer allows for ties, draws are also acceptable in some ba' games—though the rough-and-tumble elements of festival football are apparent in those situations. For example, in one nineteenth-century Scottish game, a handba' was split in two, giving both sides a little taste of victory. The tie was likely later celebrated over another festival football tradition: drinking many pints of beer.

STATS AND FACTS

Dimensions: The balls vary in size from the extremely large (27 inches in diameter, weighing 4 pounds) to relatively small (3.43 inches in diameter, but weighing a hefty 1 pound, 4 ounces). One midsized ball has a diameter of 8.9 inches and weighs nearly 3 pounds.

Royal Treatment: The English town of Ashborne has the most regal affair. It received the title "Royal Shrovetide Football" in 1922 after the town sent a specially decorated football to London in honor of the marriage of King George V's daughter Mary on Shrove Tuesday. Since then, the Prince of Wales has traveled to the hamlet twice to start festivities by throwing in the ball. In 1928, the future King Edward VIII offered up the ball, and in 2003, Prince Charles, holding the ball, was carried in on shoulders (a tradition for the guest, but one that Edward didn't accept).

Language: Each team in a festival football match commonly has a name. The most typical are the *Uppies* and the *Downies* (or *Doonies* in Scotland), as most matches pit those at the top of a harbor town against those lower down closer to the water.

Bandy ball

Though some may scratch their head today when told there's a sport called bandy, the game was popular enough in Shakespeare's day that the Bard mentioned it in *Romeo and Juliet*. Romeo takes time from his personal

drama to point out that "bandying" has been outlawed in the streets of Verona.

Back in the day, the rules differed throughout Europe—sometimes players would shoot at a goal, while others would aim for holes (golf style). Generally speaking, it was played with a curved stick, and the balls, which also came in all different sizes, were typically made of leather or wood (the knob or gnarls of a tree trunk sculpted into an orb being a particular favorite).

The Victorian British penchant for rule making brought the sport into the modern age. With shallow marshes that froze quickly in cold weather, the English town of Bury Fen was an ideal place to slap on the skates and glide around. Locals searching for a little more competition figured bandy would be particularly fun on ice, starting what was effectively a skating variation of field hockey. In the late nineteenth century, Bury Fen bandy organizers set up rules, giving the ball very exact specifications. The regulations required a solid, tough India rubber sphere that was about the size of a tennis ball. Usually red, the sphere was dubbed *the cat* by its inventors. A durable orb was necessary as the sport was played outdoors on wide, often uneven, open tracts of ice. Today, Bandy is played on a surface that is 110 yards long and 60 yards wide with players skating some 7 to 11 miles per 90-minute game.

The Bury Fen men worked diligently to spread their sport and succeeded in catching favor with royalty throughout Northern Europe. The Princess of Wales reportedly played the game (though she likely used a tennis ball rather than the heavier cat as competing with a lighter sphere was the custom for women). One source claimed that the Swedish royal family was among the game's first players in that country. Bandy was also introduced in Holland, Switzerland, Germany, Russia, Norway, and Finland between 1890 and 1910.

In most of those locales, the game didn't stick with the notable exceptions of the Baltic and Scandinavian regions. In particular, bandy caught on in Russia and Sweden, where the game remains big business today. Top professional Russian players can earn up to $500,000 a season, while Swedish television broadcasts bandy games.

With so much at stake in that region, the cat did receive a serious makeover in the 1990s. It was jumbo-sized from its original dimensions, increasing in diameter by about 25 percent. The reason: Swedish organizers believed a larger ball would be better for TV viewers, according to bandy official Magnus Sköld. The bigger ball may have made a difference on camera, but it became worryingly easy to curve the ball or knock it at breakneck speeds. In a drama that wasn't quite Shakespearean, the players complained and it was returned to its original Victorian dimensions.

STATS AND FACTS

Dimensions: An official ball, which is orange and has a hard, thick, ridged outer plastic shell (to help get spin on the ball), is approximately 2.5 inches in diameter and weighs between 2.1 and 2.3 ounces.

Speed: Although there's a long-standing rule that prevents sticks from being lifted above the shoulder when smacking the ball, the cat can reach velocities of more than 100 miles per hour.

From Russia with Love: A Russian version of bandy dates back hundreds of years before its introduction from the British. Peter the Great (1672–1725) was supposedly an avid supporter of the game. In Russia, the modern game is known as *ball hockey* or *Russian hockey*.

Language: The term *bandy* comes from the Teutonic word *bandja*, which means "a curved stick." One usage for *bandy* is as a verb, meaning "to exchange (as in words or actions) either in an argumentative or light and casual manner." This definition stems from the actual knocking around of a ball with bandies. It was used in its harshest manner in Shakespeare's *King Lear*, when Lear asks Oswald, "Do you bandy looks with me, you rascal?" before striking him.

Baseball

If you want to understand the history of baseball, follow the ball. Scholars dubbed the low-scoring early years of the game as the *dead-ball era*. When Babe Ruth made the move from pitcher to hitter and began bopping balls out of sight at big-league games, we moved into the *live-ball era*. And more recently, starting in the 1990s, when the number of those balls leaving the stadium reached astronomical proportions, experts wondered whether we were in the *juiced-ball era*. (With the last one, it turned out the players, not the baseballs, were juiced. Check your encyclopedia under the heading *Congressional steroids hearings, baseball*, for more information.)

Despite their importance in the lexicon of the sport, baseballs in their early days were made in quite a haphazard fashion. The sport's roots primarily come from

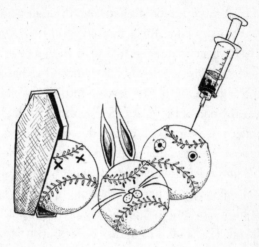

the British Isles, where rudimentary bat and ball games stoolball and rounders (they both feature pitching and hitting but are not nearly as complicated as baseball) and the more advanced cricket were all played before the development of baseball. Despite having potential ball prototypes from those games, baseballs were anything but uniform before the late 1850s. In big cities such as New York, cobblers were employed to cut up old shoes for the sphere's center and cover them up with leather or sheepskin. Giving a different meaning to the advice "Keep your eye on the ball," the eyeballs of sturgeon, which are apparently surprisingly flexible, were used as the core for balls in the lake regions. These early balls looked nothing like those at ballparks today. One popular variation was called the *lemon peel* ball. It was made of a single piece of leather with two sets of perpendicular stitches that created an *X* shape on one end of the ball. The nickname came from the fact that it looked as if the ball could be peeled back in four sections like a fruit. Regardless of the outer design, these early varieties did all have one thing in common: They were extra large. Rules written up in 1857 required balls to have a circumference of 10 to 10.25 inches, making them more like small softballs than modern baseballs.

As the game started to develop into a national pastime at the end of the nineteenth century, the ball took its modern shape and size. In fact, dimensions set in 1872 are practically the same as those used today. The two-piece *figure eight*–designed cover, which is still used on current balls, was so popular that multiple people took credit for its invention. Proving that no argument is too small, a debate continues to rage in Massachusetts over whether the town of Stoughton's Ellis Drake or the hamlet of Natick's Colonel William Cutler did the trick. Whoever deserves the honor, it appears that the figure eight first started becoming the go-to style when early baseball manufacturer William Harwood, who, like Culter, was from Natick, began mass-producing them in 1858.

Increased interest in the game led other entrepreneurs to ratchet up production. A. J. Reach, one of the first baseball-making magnates, had a factory with 300 workers constructing balls in 1890. They were paid by the piece (average salary: $10 to $15 per week), and a top worker could produce about three dozen balls in a day. Big business meant going abroad to find the best materials. At one point, the Russian horsehide industry actually held sway over the baseball market. In the years preceding the Russian Revolution, the hides of Tartar horses were deemed essential for making top-notch baseballs. Between 1911 and 1915, U.S. captains of industry warned that relations with Russians needed to remain cordial or else the strong and durable horsehide would no longer be available. Though it's unclear, one would expect that an alternative was found after the rise of communism.

Even with all these efforts put into ball making, the initial results were a bit of a dud. The rubber-cored ball would get worn and lumpy during the game. In part, the problem had to do with the custom of keeping base-balls in the contest as long as possible. As a result, teams generally had their best chance at scoring in the early innings before the ball softened. You know things were tough when Frank Baker earned the nickname "Home Run" during this period and never hit more than 12 homers in a season—that's 61 fewer than the current record. And Frank was lucky; after hitting just 6 dingers in his first two full seasons, the slugger benefited from a new cork-centered sphere that became a fixture following its use at the 1910 World Series. With more hop, some journalists dubbed it the *rabbit ball*.

Fans really began believing something strange was stuffed into balls in 1920. That year, Babe Ruth hit 54 homers—25 more than the game's previous best. Everybody looked to the ball. In a 1921 *Baseball Magazine* article, representatives from the Cleveland Indians, Brooklyn Dodgers, and Pittsburgh Pirates were all convinced that a livelier ball was in play. Conspiracy theorists believed a springier sphere was clandestinely introduced in order to make the sport more exciting and lure disappointed fans to games following the famed "Black Sox" gambling scandal (members of the 1919 Chicago White Sox allegedly threw the World Series). No proof ever supported this contention, though a new cushioned cork-centered ball was officially introduced in the mid-1920s, which probably did increase home runs.

Maybe all the commotion led makers to lie low because little changed with the ball over the following decades other than a switch from horsehide to cowhide covers in the 1970s. One exception was during World War II when a rubber shortage required the use of a Malaysian gum substance called *balata*. The balls proved a colossal failure and were quickly discarded.

But ball-based conspiracy theories never seem to completely go away. In the late 1990s, home run totals skyrocketed yet again and everyone pointed to the balls. Later, when it was discovered that players taking performance-enhancing drugs were the likelier culprit for the homer frenzy, some suggested that baseball executives in the know about steroids floated the idea of a juiced ball as a red herring. Again, there was no evidence to support the claim. Nevertheless, it was a reminder that when things change in baseball, the first place people look is at the ball.

STATS AND FACTS

Dimensions: The circumference is between 9 and 9.25 inches, and it weighs 5 ounces (give or take a quarter of an ounce).

Colors: Though new baseballs are often referred to as *pearls* because of their smooth white hue, the idea of having colored baseballs has been a point of contention on several occasions throughout baseball's history. In 1870, a company called Peck & Snyder introduced the dark blood-colored "Dead Red Ball." The company claimed the new shade would help fielders and batters who objected to the "dazzling whiteness" of the white ball on a sunny day. In 1928, two minor league teams experimented with a yellow ball. A decade later similar trials occurred at the Major League level, but nothing ever came of the effort. In the 1970s, maverick Oakland A's owner Charles Finley pushed for hot-orange baseballs to help batters see the ball at night, but he was also shot down.

Variations: Ironically, though baseball, in part, owes its roots to the British sport of rounders, when it comes to the modern ball, rounders follows baseball. The rounders sphere is lighter and softer than a baseball but uses the same figure eight design and stitching as the American invention. Welsh baseball, another similar British game, also patterns its sphere after the baseball.

Humidor: With less humidity, balls fly faster out of stadiums at higher altitudes. As one would suspect, Coors Field in the mile-high city of Denver immediately became a home run hitter's dream when the Colorado Rockies joined the Major Leagues in 1993. After years of demoralized pitchers, the Rockies came up with a way to lessen the impact of its location: Bring the humidity directly to the balls. In 2002, the club set up a humidor, where balls get their own personal sauna before game time. It worked as the stadium has since cut down on its annual home run totals.

Strange But True: A minor league baseball player once used a potato as a baseball substitute to trick a runner. In 1987, Rick Lundblade of the Reading (Pa.) Phillies was on third base when he thought he saw the opposing catcher make an errant throw by him in the middle of a game. He immediately scampered on home, but was surprised to find Williamsport (Pa.) Bills' catcher Dave Bresnahan holding an actual baseball in his hand. It turned out that Bresnahan had carved a potato to look like a baseball and had snuck it onto the field, throwing it into the outfield to deceive Lundblade. Bresnahan was pulled from the game and Williamsport's parent club, the Cleveland Indians, released him from his contract the next day. As for the spud, it's part of the permanent collection (in a jar of denatured alcohol) at the Baseball Reliquary in Southern California.

Language: Baseballs thrown at high velocities have been popular fodder for nicknames. The media used to call a speeding fastball an *aspirin tablet* because it looked more like the little white headache elixir than a ball when thrown at blistering speeds. (Playing off the nickname, a pitcher once quipped that an aspirin tablet was "the best way for a pitcher to cure his manager's headache.") A little more generically, the ball has also been referred to as the *pill*.

Basketball

On the playground, the game of basketball is known as hoops. But when James Naismith invented the sport on a cold December day in 1891, he was more concerned about the ball than the location where points would be scored.

A physical education teacher at a Young Men's Christian Association college in Springfield, Massachusetts, Naismith taught a class of eighteen aspiring YMCA

administrators and was stumped for activities when winter came. He had little to offer indoors other than calisthenics, gymnastics, and some children's games. He tried modifying such popular pastimes as rugby and soccer for the gym with little success before finally reaching his eureka moment.

The night before introducing basketball, he set out a list of thirteen rules for a game intended to embody nonviolent Christian ideals and, at the same time, offer rigorous activity. In outlining the sport, the ball weighed heavily on Naismith's mind. Nine of his regulations discussed the ball; only five mentioned the goal. He would tell the *New York Times* in 1902 that the right ball was essential to make the sport "scientific and interesting." It had to be large enough to be "handled with the hands and not hidden." Based on these parameters, the original orb of choice was a soccer ball.

Once he had settled on the ball, figuring out what to do with it was the next task. To avoid the violence of football, players would be prevented from running with the ball, and to sidestep the jostling in soccer, there would be no kicking. The participants were also prohibited from punching the ball with their fists or physically tussling for the ball. Only then did Naismith appear to focus on the goals, which were erected vertically in order to prevent damage in gyms and to further encourage finesse in passing and throwing. The first hoops, which were nailed to a track 10 feet above the gym floor, were actually peach baskets because boxes couldn't be found (hence the name *basketball* rather than *boxball*).

The first match ended with the unsexy score of 1–0. On the plus side, the players had to retrieve the ball only once from a basket because nobody thought to cut out the bottom of the baskets (a hoop in which the ball could fully pass through didn't come into use until 1906). With students in the class from all over the United States (and some from Canada), the game spread quickly, first becoming a staple at YMCA gyms and then among colleges and secular clubs. A testament to the game's embrace was the speed at which a sport-specific sphere was developed to replace the soccer ball. Within three years of Naismith's introduction, the first basketball was produced. It was about 4 inches larger in circumference than the soccer ball—and about the same weight as today's basketball.

In those early years, a contentious ball-related controversy had to do with bouncing (aka dribbling). Though a key part of the sport today—the ball is dribbled some 1,700 times during an average 40-minute college game—it was a no-no in the formative years as some organizers thought it encouraged rough, selfish play. What this ilk wanted was a game emphasizing passing the ball downcourt instead of one player taking control with the dribble. Until 1915, a player who dribbled the ball was prohibited from also shooting it. Instead, the athlete was required to dish it off to a teammate. Even as late as 1929, some coaches tried but failed to outlaw the maneuver.

Dribbling certainly didn't help the early basketball, which tended to get lumpy or deaden from the impact (laces on the top of the ball also probably didn't provide for a smooth dribble). "The hardest thing was to keep the ball round," college coaching great John Wooden once recalled, reminiscing about playing in 1918. "We usually had to tie a rubber band around it to hold its shape." Thankfully, by the early 1940s, molded basketballs were developed, ending the need for laces and providing a more uniform bounce. The ball was also being shaped into its current size during this era—an official basketball was 2 inches smaller in circumference than the inaugural ball, according to rules established when the National Basketball Association (NBA) commenced in 1949.

As the size of players increased, regulations came and went controlling what these big men could do with the basketball. One that stuck: In the late 1950s, touching the ball while it was in the hoop or above the cylinder (known as goaltending) was outlawed. One that didn't: College basketball prohibited slam-dunking in 1968. The rule makers came to their senses in 1977, reinstituting the play.

Another big issue in the mid-twentieth century was ball color. In the first half of the century, the ball was typically a tan hue—although a yellow ball was sometimes used. Tan was eventually overthrown by the iconic orange in the late 1950s. Butler University coach Tony Hinkle was credited with bringing it to the college ranks in 1958. The brighter ball was tested at the 1958 NCAA Finals in Louisville, Kentucky, and adopted as an easier color for players and fans to follow.

Ball color returned to center court when the American Basketball Association (ABA) formed in 1967 to compete with the NBA. The ABA introduced a red, white, and blue ball, in order to appeal to both television audiences and women (it's unclear why they thought a bright ball would dazzle the ladies). The league guarded their patriotic sphere jealously, suing prominent ball maker AMF Voit when it copied the color scheme. The courts rejected the ABA's copyright infringement claim, saying the ball was sort of like a tennis tube sock—the sock is still just a sock and cannot be trademarked just because it has a red, white, and blue band around the top. Ultimately, the bright ball was ditched when the ABA and the NBA merged in 1976.

In the twenty-first century, playability has emerged as a main concern. Since its inception, the NBA basketball had been a pretty static sphere. The only substantial change was a shift from a four-paneled to an eight-paneled ball in 1970. But in 2006, the league decided to throw out the old leather ball and replace it with a high-technology composite microfiber version. The newly designed balls also ditched the traditional eight oblong panel look for two interlocking, cross-shaped panels. The upshot was a ball that was supposed to supply superior grip and feel.

It turned out to be a big mistake. Shaquille O'Neal compared it to a toy store model, and Steve Nash said it caused finger cuts and burns. The players' union went so far as to file an unfair labor practice grievance against the league. Physicists at the University of Texas–Arlington even did a study claiming the ball bounced 30 percent more erratically than the old leather ball. Within two months of the ball's introduction, the NBA got the picture and dropped the high-tech sphere. John McLendon, a Naismith student in the 1930s, told a *Boston Globe* reporter in 1991 that the game's inventor desired the sport to be for the players and not those off the court. At least when it comes to the ball, Naismith may have gotten his wish.

STATS AND FACTS

Dimenisons: A full-sized men's ball is between 9.39 and 9.55 inches in diameter and weighs between 20 and 22 ounces. The balls come slightly smaller in the women's game: 9.07 to 9.23 inches and 17.5 to 19.5 ounces.

Bounceability: The right spring in a ball is essential. A standard professional basketball dropped from a 6-foot height must be able to bounce about 70 percent of the way back (between 49 and 54 inches). That requires between 7.5 and 8.5 pounds of air per square inch in the ball.

Inspiration: Naismith vaguely based basketball on a game he played as child in Canada called *duck on a rock*.

The aim was to lob rocks at a target from 20 feet away. It required a soft touch that Naismith wanted to bring to basketball.

Big Business: In 2008, $167 million worth of basketballs were sold in the United States; that's nearly double the amount spent on footballs ($89 million) and more than three times the total for baseballs ($49 million).

Language: The tiny bumps used for better gripping on the surface of a basketball are called *pebbles*. There are more than 31,000 of them on an official NBA ball.

Beach ball

The ancient Greeks didn't have beach blankets or bikinis, but that didn't stop them from enjoying the age-old tradition of playing ball and frolicking on sandy shores. In Homer's *Odyssey*, the sixth book talks about Princess Nausicaa and her companions going down to the beach to do some laundry. Once the washing was done, they had a picnic and then "the princess and her retinue threw their veils to the wind, [and] struck up a game of ball."

Some 2,500 years after those literary beginnings, the ball began taking shape as the oversized, light, colorful orb we know today. That journey started in Southern California, where a new rubber company was looking to diversify their product line. In 1922, W. J. Voit founded Voit Rubber (later named AMF Voit). Initially, his company made tire retreading products, but Voit moved into the sporting goods field by creating what is likely the first inflatable rubber beach ball. It's quite possible Voit was not alone in early production as a photo from a Wash-

ington, DC, department store circa 1921 or 1922 seems to show multipaneled, multicolored beach balls hanging from the rafters. But it's pretty clear Voit was the first to popularize the sphere meant for the sun and the surf.

How did these bright balls enter the public consciousness? For whatever reason, companies believed beach balls were a valuable marketing vehicle for attracting customers. In a 1924 *Los Angeles Times* advertisement, Harris & Frank department store offered "a big, light, sea-going ball" if a customer purchased any knicker suit at its boys' department. The *L.A. Times* must have found this type of inducement a smart business practice because during the 1930s the company gave a beach ball to any child who could persuade a friend or family member to buy a two-month *Times* subscription.

During this era, the beach ball made a splash in the popular culture as well. It became an omnipresent prop for beachside images of bathing suit–clad women. While these pictures tended to be photographs, even Pablo Picasso got involved with his 1932 cubist painting *Bather with Beach Ball* (albeit, Picasso depicted a relatively undersized white ball).

By the 1940s, the composition of beach balls was changing from rubber to a soft, durable plastic. In 1947, the famed Chicago department store Marshall Fields advertised a "gaily colored" plastic beach ball for $4. It boasted that this orb was leakproof with welded seams. A much better deal was offered two years later in Chicago by Stineway's stores, which sold a "vinylite plastic" beach ball for a mere 28 cents.

Some companies continued to sell rubber—or latex rubber—balls, but by the 1960s, the super-light plastic ball with six alternating colorful panels (usually some combination of red, white, blue, and yellow) became the norm thanks to a slew of surf films. These movies—most notably the Annette Funicello–Frankie Avalon flicks—featured scantily clad teenagers who seemingly loved to dance and play nonstop with the iconic beach ball.

Eventually, these balls migrated inland from the oceanside. In the 1970s, fans started smuggling beach balls into stadiums. The balls were inflated and then smacked around. Baseball spectators at Dodger Stadium in Los Angeles were early adopters of this beach ball mania. A 1975 *Pasadena Star News* report lamented how multiple beach balls in the stands dominated attention despite a Dodgers 5–0 victory over the Atlanta Braves. Still, L.A. starting pitcher Don Sutton had a sense of humor about the distraction. "At least I got my hands on two beach balls that floated down—and my youngsters will have them in the morning," he quipped.

Not all teams find beach balls funny. In fact, the Los Angeles Angels of Anaheim strictly prohibit bringing the balls into its ballpark. In truth, the Angels may be on to something as devotees of England's Liverpool FC soccer club found out in October 2009. A sixteen-year-old whacked a large inflated beach ball onto the field during an English Premier League match between Liverpool and Sunderland. The light plastic orb hit the game ball just as a Sunderland player was shooting, deflecting the soccer ball into Liverpool's goal. It was the game's only score, giving the underdog Sunderland club a 1–0 win. While the teenager was lustily booed, the beach ball fared well after the debacle. It was purchased at auction for £411.77 (about $687) and now sits in the National Football Museum in Preston, England, likely making it the world's most famous beach ball.

STATS AND FACTS

Dimensions: Sizes vary greatly, but an 18-inch diameter ball (when inflated) tends to be the most popular. It weighs 4 ounces. Buyers can pick up balls as large as 17 feet and 45 pounds at a cost of $899.95, according to Dave Layton at www.beachballs.com.

Language: *Polyvinyl chloride* (better known as PVC) is the soft pliable form of plastic that is the industry standard for constructing beach balls.

Bearing balls (ball bearings)

Some may scoff at the idea of bearing balls being included in a book about sports and recreation balls. After all, these micro-sized spheres aren't the center of any game. You don't throw, hit, or catch them—unless you count the pinball, which is a large version of the orb. And yet these pint-sized spheres may be one of the most broadly influential balls in sports and games. (Geek note: They are officially called bearing balls and the mechanical contraption they work in is the *ball bearing*.) In the movie *Fletch*, Chevy Chase offered the classic line: "It's all ball bearings nowadays." He's not far from the truth. There are at least a half dozen pastimes—ranging from bicycling to flinging the yo-yo—that can directly credit ball bearings for what they are today.

The idea of using ball bearings to make the mechanical movement of objects more efficient reaches back to at least the Romans. Leonardo da Vinci began writing about the mechanical device around 1500. More than a century later, Galileo added to the intellectual discourse when he wrote about captured or *caged* ball bearings. Keeping the balls from uncontrollably rolling around would help avoid the friction, which minimized the effectiveness of the bearings. But it wasn't until the end of the nineteenth century that industrially made balls with uniform size began changing the landscape of sports and recreation.

No sport was transformed more than bicycling. In order to get pedals smoothly running, bearings were lubricated and placed in grooves called *races*. All of a sudden people could cruise along at nearly three times the average walking speed. Bike races had begun before ball bearings were added to bicycle design, but proliferated afterward. Understanding the value of ball bearings, bike mechanics integrated them into other important advancements. For example, the Wright brothers, who were bicycle repairman by trade, used ball bearings in the first airplane, the Wright Flyer.

The silky moves were not limited to bicycles and early planes. Ball bearings made roller skating a popular pastime and revolutionized the art of fly-fishing. The reel used to create slack on the line and then pull in a fish could spin with considerably less effort thanks to the little balls in the bearing. Although steel was typically chosen to make the minispheres, some expert fishermen opted for bronze or even small jewels (such as agate) for their bearing balls, believing they would hold up better. Elsewhere, ball bearings played a part in cleaning up rowing. For years, competitive rowers would grease their pants so that they could move back and forth while propelling their boat with oars. Sliding seats changed that messy movement in the final decades of the nineteenth century. Wheels using ball bearings became a part of seat designs.

An unlikely beneficiary of the ball bearing revolution has been yo-yos. These toys date back to antiquity, but got a considerable upgrade in the mid-1980s. Ball bearings allow the yo-yo to spin at hyperspeed, which opened up the way for never-before-contemplated tricks. It has also turned yo-yoing into a contact sport. Members of the yo-yo community are known to share descriptions of their battle scars on the Internet. Among the ball-bearing-fueled yo-yo injuries: burst blood vessels, chipped teeth, and badly bruised hands.

STATS AND FACTS

Dimensions: Sizes can vary greatly. One type of ball bearing that is used as ammunition in BB guns is 0.177 inch in diameter and weighs 0.002 ounce.

Manufacture: Balls typically start out as thick cords of steel and are then cut down, shaped, and polished in a process that takes at least 8 hours.

Language: When it comes to BB guns, the *BB* does not stand for "bearing balls" or "ball bearings." Instead, it refers to the type of lead shot (in between B- and BBB-sized ammo) originally used with the air-loaded guns. In 1928, top BB gun sellers Daisy Manufacturing Co. redesigned their guns and began using steel bearing balls for their firearms.

Billiard ball (snooker ball)

Take a look around the room. Wherever you see plastic, you can thank the sport of billiards. Quite simply, plastics are a direct descendant of centuries of frustration over the shape and consistency of billiard balls. Billiards' modern history dates back to at least the reign of France's Louis XI (1461–1483) and was also a part of Elizabethan

England's popular culture. William Shakespeare made reference to the sport in *Anthony and Cleopatra*, and Mary Queen of Scots was such an adherent to billiards that she insisted on having a table during the time she was jailed while awaiting her execution in 1587.

Even in her precarious state, Mary probably complained about her table's carved wooden balls because, for all these early players, reliably consistent balls were elusive. The problem: It was extremely difficult to fashion the wood into completely round spheres. They would also split over time and would change shape easily, expanding in a warm environment.

Innovation initially came in the most unfortunate way. In the 1600s, balls constructed of ivory became the standard. Unlike their wooden predecessors, these balls could be shaped far more easily into a perfect orb. Players could also enjoy that iconic click noise as balls caromed off each other. Of course, the ivory came at a very steep price. In a single year, 10,000 or more elephants could be slaughtered to meet the worldwide demand for these ivory spheres.

Ultimately, ivory was an imperfect upgrade. Like the wood versions, ivory orbs could chip and crack and would change shape as the temperature shifted. Five minutes in 10-degree temperatures and ivory balls would be ruined. While the homes of the elite didn't have to worry about such frigid situations, climate control was of paramount concern. Heated bumpers in the days before the invention of vulcanized rubber were quite common. Even Queen Victoria used a heated billiard table to keep her balls from warping. No matter what the effort, over time, balls would end up shaped more like an egg than an orb. In Gilbert and Sullivan's famed comic opera *The Mikado*, the Mikado sings of the worst fate for a billiards player. It included playing with "elliptical billiard balls."

One would like to believe that conscience led to the move away from ivory, but it was more an issue of economy. The fear that a supply of ivory would run out led the New York billiards manufacturer Phelan & Collender to offer a $10,000 reward in 1863 to the person who could find a reliable alternative. The amount offered was quite substantial because the task was not easy. Dozens of attempts from rubber to porcelain all failed.

Although it took six years, a printer from Albany, New York, named John Wesley Hyatt finally took the honors with a breakthrough that not only changed billiard balls but also ushered in the plastics age. Hyatt's invention was a synthetic material created by dissolving nitrocellulose in a series of solvents and combining it with camphor. Called *celluloid*, it became the first commercially viable plastic.

Hyatt's balls were introduced to the marketplace with much fanfare in the 1870s, but they had problems of their own. The balls were quite flammable and some ivory supporters even claimed they would set off a small explosion if they collided too hard. According to a popular story, one of the balls' field testers was a saloon owner in Colorado. He reported that when a billiard player in his establishment accidentally touched a ball with a lighted cigar, the combination led to a small bang, causing every man in the room to draw his gun.

These artificial *composition* balls, as they were known, found buyers, but they were unable to completely supplant the traditional ivory. As late as 1920, billiards experts still insisted that ivory was the only true material for pure billiards aficionados, and one company made a new $50,000 offer for an even better ivory substitute. Thankfully, plastics continued to make strides after Hyatt's initial breakthrough. Eventually, balls made of a less explosive plastic known as *cast phelonic resin* fully replaced ivory and remains the material of choice today.

While the plastic solution is a tremendous legacy for billiards, its ivory past is not. Balls were certainly not the only use for ivory, but their manufacture contributed to an African elephant population decline from nearly 10 million 500 years ago to approximately

300,000 to 500,000 at the beginning of the twenty-first century.

STATS AND FACTS

Dimensions: Different sizes of balls are used for different games. Pool balls are 2.25 inches in diameter (with 0.005-inch plus or minus leeway) and weigh 5.5 to 6 ounces. Snooker, an English variation, uses slightly smaller balls (2.0625 inches in diameter; a weight of 5 to 5.5 ounces).

More on Snooker: Snooker became a popular British pastime in the late nineteenth century. Eight red balls are racked in a manner similar to eight ball, and six assorted colored balls (yellow, green, brown, blue, pink, and black) are lined up at other locations on the table. A player must alternate hitting in a red ball and another colored ball. Each of the nonred balls has a different value. In the late 1960s, the sport was actually saved by television. When BBC started its new Technicolor television network, BBC2, in 1969, it wanted programming that would shine brightly. With its multicolored balls, snooker was chosen and a show called *Pot Black* made the game popular again.

Language: There is some controversy over the roots of the word *billiard*. French in origin, the word comes from either the term for the wooden cue stick—the *billart*— or the word *bille*, which means a "little ball." *Pool* has a simpler explanation: It comes from the French term *poule*, which means "pool" in English. A gambling game from the beginning, the pool was the pot where wagers were kept.

BALL PHRASES

The ball has given so much to the English language. Below are thirteen idiomatic expressions featuring the ball. Admittedly, I cheated a bit on number 5 (*have a ball*) as it comes from the dance rather than the sphere.

1. *A whole new ball game*: A new or changed situation.
2. *Behind the eight ball*: In a difficult position.
3. *Carry the ball forward*: To do work necessary to advance a project or activity.
4. *Drop the ball*: Failing in a task; making a mistake.
5. *Have a ball*: Have a great time.
6. *In the ballpark (In the same ballpark)*: Closing in on a resolution or agreement.
7. *Keep the ball rolling (Get the ball rolling)*: To maintain momentum (to begin a project or activity).
8. *Oddball*: A person or object that is strange or eccentric.
9. *On the ball (keeping your eye on the ball)*: Being on top of a matter.
10. *Playing ball (play ball)*: A willingness to engage in an activity or cooperate with another (sometimes against your better judgment).
11. *Playing hardball*: To act in a determined way to achieve one's goal that often includes ignoring niceties.
12. *That's the way the ball bounces*: The matter is out of your control; that's life.
13. *The ball is in your court*: It's your move.

While nearly all these phrases are derived directly from sports, *keep the ball rolling* has political roots. During the 1840 presidential campaign between William Henry Harrison and Martin Van Buren, Harrison supporters actually rolled huge balls (between 10

continues . . .

. . . continued from previous page

and 12 feet in diameter) covered with slogans down streets from town to town in support of their candidate. While it's unclear whether this was the first time the phrase was used, these efforts to keep the ball rolling for Harrison popularized the expression.

Lest you think that ball phrases are only for the English-speaking world, there are examples of other languages using them for idiomatic means. In Russian, "пробний шар" (*probny shar*) means "trial balloon," but literally translates into "probe ball."

Bocce balls

The Italians have given us so much: pizza, a leaning tower, Chianti, and oh yes, some of the world's greatest artists and thinkers. But in the ball world, the country's widest-reaching legacy is *bocce*.

The concept of tossing a ball in an attempt to get closest to a target dates back to the Egyptians. The Greeks were also known to play a similar game. (Greek doctors thought it was a "restorative activity.") But the Romans brought passion to the game. It is said that Roman soldiers enjoyed bocce whenever they had a break from fighting Carthage during the Punic Wars. Later, Emperor Augustus was a player, giving the sport an air of nobility. Enthusiasm for the game was such that just about anything could properly serve as a ball. Rocks were the original projectile, but Romans also used coconuts obtained in Africa before eventually settling on a hard olive wood for construction.

Roman imperialism was good for bocce as centurions and foot soldiers alike spread the game while conquering large swaths of Europe. Locals then put their own touches on the game. The French went with *pétanque* (see page 114), and the English opted for lawn bowling (see page 82). A primary difference with these variations was a distinctive type of ball (the French fancied metal spheres, while the British went with an unevenly weighted orb).

Through the rise and fall of the Roman Empire, the Renaissance (Galileo enjoyed bocce), the country's unification (Italian folk hero Giuseppe Garibaldi was an expert), and even fascism (Benito Mussolini attempted to co-opt the sport), the game has remained a staple of Italian culture. But the balls have changed during this long stretch. Modern bocce balls are now perfectly round and made of a hard synthetic plastic about the size of a large softball (a small plastic or wood target ball—called a *pallino*—is about the size of a golf ball).

STATS AND FACTS

Dimensions: The larger balls are 4.5 inches in diameter and weigh 2.2 pounds. The *pallino* varies in weight and is normally 1.375 to 2.5 inches in diameter.

Language: *Bocce* is the plural of *boccia*, which means "ball." It comes from *bottia*, the Vulgar Latin word for "boss." Presumably, the involvement of the likes of Emperor Augustus gave the game its name—or possibly, it's because the round projectile was in charge.

Bowling ball

Fred Flintstone would have never employed his own personal chemist to improve his bowling ball. The idea seems more outlandish than his twinkle-toes delivery.

Then again if he'd been a professional bowler in the 1970s, he probably wouldn't have thought twice. Although bowling is historically considered a working-class game (think *The Honeymooners'* Ralph Kramden), its ball has undergone the type of changes that only a PhD could fully appreciate.

The sport dates back to the Egyptians, who hurled stone spheres at pins more than 5,000 years ago. By AD 300, Germans were playing with the pins representing heathens and the ball presumably the power of the righteous. Considering that fact, it might not be a surprise that the great religious reformer Martin Luther was apparently an avid bowler. The game came to the United States via German and Dutch settlers and emerged as a popular pastime in the nineteenth century. Washington Irving's famous 1819 tale *Rip Van Winkle* even talks about a nine-pin contest. As the century wore on, bowling gained a reputation as a gambling game. Legend has it that the move to ten pins occurred in 1841 when Connecticut authorities outlawed the lascivious nine-pin game. Organizers responded by adding a tenth pin to circumvent the law.

By this period, stone had been replaced by the toughest of woods—*lignum vitae*—as the essential ball-making material. Shipped from Puerto Rico or South America, the balls were specially treated to handle the cooler climate. When properly oiled, the wood bowling sphere could handle the punishment of knocking down pins night after night. Still, getting a perfectly round and evenly weighted ball was nearly impossible.

True science made its entry into the bowling ball world at the dawn of the twentieth century. In 1905, a rubber concoction called the *Evertrue* supplanted the wooden standard. Shaping vulcanized rubber into something that could roll down an alley was no easy task. It required a special process to ensure the material had an even weight and hardness in order to prevent uneven wearing. The new ball provided more dependability, but its moment in the spotlight was short-lived. Less than a decade later, Brunswick, best known at the time as a billiards manufacturer, unveiled the *Mineralite* ball. The company backed up its invention with a savvy sense of marketing. The Mineralite had a "mysterious rubber compound," Brunswick claimed, and was ambitiously sent around the world on an 8.5-month sales tour. Exhibitions were set up in such bustling metropolises as

London, Berlin, Paris, Rome, Bombay, Manila, and Hong Kong. The Mineralite remained the industry standard for nearly a half-century.

Appropriately, just as disco was becoming popular in the 1970s, polyester offered scientists a new substance to work with. Balls made of polyester allowed bowlers to cut through the oil used on lanes, providing a straighter shot. (Stylistically, players could match their balls with their shirts.) With different consistencies and materials—hard or soft, plastic or rubber—professional players would lug at least five spheres to every tournament in order to have the right ball for the right situation.

But the variety wasn't enough for one enterprising pro, who further pushed technological boundaries. Don McCune was a middling player on the pro bowlers' tour when he began tinkering with his bowling balls. Looking for an advantage, he consulted a chemist about ways to soften up his ball. While the harder polyester spheres were good for straight shots, he wanted a super-soft option that he could hook with more accuracy than those on the market. The pair discovered that if a typical rubber bowling ball was soaked in a chemical solvent called toluene, it would soften so much that it would grip better on an oily lane. In 1974, McCune began going from town to town with a bucketful of toluene. The results were impressive: That season, he won six tournaments, led the tour in money earnings, and was named player of the year.

When word got out about McCune's *soaker* process, other bowlers followed. At one event in Redwood City, California, 160 bowlers were filling up their bathtubs and buckets with toluene. This concerned local fire officials, who shut down the amateur chemists for fear that the highly volatile solvent might combust. The Professional Bowlers Association banned McCune's soaking efforts and set specific standards for ball hardness. There is leeway, but ultra-soft balls, like the ones devised by McCune, are prohibited.

Only mildly deterred, lab mavens continued making breakthroughs (but within the rules). In the 1980s, urethane balls offered more precision and durability. The next step was reactive urethane. Computer calibrated, these babies, which remain popular today, have an internal weight that can be balanced to the needs of each individual bowler. Now that's the type of ball Fred Flintstone could enjoy.

STATS AND FACTS

Dimensions: 8.5 inches in diameter (a 0.095-inch variation is allowed); the ball must weigh less than 16 pounds (there is no minimum weight, but the lightest ball at the local alley tends to be 6 pounds).

Variations: Candlepin and duckpin bowling use smaller balls and different pins (candlepins are skinny; duckpins are squat). Duckpin balls are 5 inches in diameter and can't weigh more than 3 pounds, 12 ounces, and candlepin balls are slightly smaller.

Language: In light of the ball advances, the Professional Bowlers Association has tried to ratchet up the difficulty for pro players. Depending on the lane conditions, the organization will use a variety of oil patterns to offset the precision of the balls. The patterns have such inviting names as the *viper, shark, scorpion, cheetah,* and *chameleon.*

Cricket ball

Winston Churchill once said: "To improve is to change; to be perfect is to change often." He certainly wasn't talking about the ball used in his country's beloved sport of

cricket. In tennis, players serving can exchange a ball on a whim. A baseball usually lasts only six or seven pitches before it's fouled off, hit out of the park, or discarded. But in test cricket, a ball has to last a minimum of 480 bowls before it can be substituted for a new one. For a little more perspective, that would be like using the same baseball for *two straight games.*

Change is a concept the lords of the cricket ball have never seemed to totally embrace. There's some debate over who actually came up with the iconic stitched seam through the equator of the cricket ball, but most historians agree it popped up between 1760 and 1775 and the design has remained since. The color has primarily stayed a cherry red (some suggest it's the best color for seeing a ball at twilight), though the recent advent of night games has led to the use of both white and pink balls.

So with all this aversion to change, is the cricket ball far from perfect as Churchill might suggest? Absolutely— but that's not necessarily a bad thing. In fact, those imperfections play a large role in shaping the sport. Strategy is often formed by the bumps and bruises the ball receives during its use. When the sphere is new and hard, teams will use a *fast bowler*, who can heave the cricket ball at high velocities on one hop and get better bounce. (Unlike their American cousin, cricket balls usually take a single hop on their way to the batter.) But when the sphere has softened, *spin bowlers*, who can take advantage of the older ball to get more movement, are typically employed.

All this unwillingness to change probably didn't bother Churchill. He wasn't a fan of the game. But he would have surely been ruffled by how players try to sidestep the natural breakdown of the ball. Churchill did once say: "In sport . . . all men must meet on equal terms." But in cricket, figuring out the best way to break the rules and illegally doctor the ball is a developing tradition. Players are allowed to polish the ball by using saliva and then wiping it off, but adding foreign substances or creating scuffs is prohibited. Old-timers believed that keeping the ball as pristine as possible was a key to success. But in recent decades, bowlers began to realize that subtle changes to the sphere could lead to far more movement. Vaseline, a soft drink bottle cap, and even a half-eaten lollipop have all been implicated in ball-tampering scandals. Apparently, sugar is a great substance for improving spin. One player admitted to sucking on a mint and then using his treacle-laden spit to help win a key match. Although Churchill was a loquacious man, I'm not sure even he has a quote relating to that one.

STATS AND FACTS

Dimensions: An official cricket ball is between 8.8125 and 9 inches in circumference and weighs 5.5 to 5.75 ounces.

Early History: The oldest written reference to cricket dates back to the late sixteenth century. It suggests that the game was played in Guildford, Surrey (located in Southeast England), during the 1550s.

Construction: In an 1853 British sporting goods catalog, cork, worsted, hemp, brown oats, suet, lard, alum, stale ale, and dragon's blood were all listed as ingredients in one manufacturer's cricket ball. Today, players settle for a tough leather exterior and a center typically made of cork-rubber composite and wool string. It can take about seventy-five days to craft a modern top-flight ball. The most painstaking part of the process involves manually compressing five layers of cork and string inside the ball.

Language: When a right-handed bowler throws a ball that hits the ground and then unexpectedly bounces to the right, it's called a *googly*. Invented by Englishman Bernard Bosanquet, the term came from a newspaper reporter who said the maneuver made onlookers' "eyes goggle." *Cricket* is said to come from an old French word *criquet*, which is defined as "a stick which serves as a target in a ball game."

Croquet balls

Croquet balls have received recognition in classic literature, spurred a presidential scandal, and been coveted by some of America's most famous authors, actors, and diplomats.

Developed in Ireland during the 1830s, the game was the toast of Victorian England. Alice's surreal croquet experience—complete with flamingo mallets and live hedgehog balls—in *Alice's Adventures in Wonderland* indicated just what cultural cachet the game possessed at the time. Within a couple of decades after its invention, croquet made it to the other side of the Atlantic. Popular among the rich in the Northeast, it garnered enough attention in American circles to get a shout-out in Louisa May Alcott's *Little Women* (published in two volumes in 1868 and 1869). It also earned an avid supporter in President Rutherford B. Hayes. His lust for the sport was so great that he diverted public funds to buy fine box-wood croquet balls, allegedly filing the purchase under the heading of "Repairs and Fuel" for the White House. A partisan uproar forced Hayes to repay the government for his quality spheres. "He could have bought a set for $10, but it was agreed that nothing but box-wood balls would answer for the White House, and they would cost six dollars more—a drain that his private fortune could never bear," his Democratic foes sarcastically wrote.

At least Hayes had good taste. The British scrutinized the best solid wood for croquet balls as if it were a science. In the beginning, differences in local bark were hotly debated. Willow and chestnut weren't up to snuff, but sycamore would do, claimed one of the game's first rule makers. Others beseeched the use of beech, while across the pond in America, maple was a popular choice. Ultimately, Turkish boxwood became the standard, as Hayes clearly understood. Proper care was also carefully considered. Experts encouraged players to rub linseed oil on balls when out of play.

Croquet lost some steam at the dawn of the twentieth century, when the finely manicured green grass spaces required for a good game were being transformed for the up-and-coming sport of lawn tennis. But the rich and famous in the United States would not be denied this leisurely pursuit. Members of the famed intellectual group the Algonquin Roundtable played, as did Washington insiders such as W. Averell Harriman. In Hollywood, superstars Humphrey Bogart and Spencer Tracy and moguls Darryl Zanuck and Sam Goldwyn enjoyed the game. Famed comedian Harpo Marx was the sport's biggest booster. He even had a specially air-conditioned room in his house to keep his croquet balls and other equipment properly acclimatized.

Balls are still made to exacting specifications, but arguments over the wood are no longer an issue. Generally speaking, they are now hollow in the center with a molding of composite elements. These materials continue to be tweaked with new forms of nylon and polyurethane being used and various groove patterns implemented for increased performance. Ironically, solid wooden balls are now the cheapest around and are used only in low-key recreational matches. (Yes, there is certainly serious croquet out there.)

STATS AND FACTS

Dimensions: Balls are 3.625 inches in diameter and weigh 16 ounces.

Ball Colors: A basic set of croquet balls has four colored balls: blue and black plays against red and yellow (pink, brown, orange, and green are used in full sets). It's unclear how those colors were determined. Current organizers can only say that "cold" colors, like blue and black, play against "hot" colors such as red and yellow. One theory is that the colors were chosen based on the dyes that were strongest and readily available during the formative days of the sport in Victorian England. An early book on the sport merely suggested: "Paint them of as many colors as there are balls. The more vivid the color, the prettier will be the effect upon the greensward, and the pleasanter the play."

Language: When croquet's first rules were published in England in 1856, *croquet* was the game's given name. The likely source for the title comes from the Irish term for the sport: *crookey*. French-sounding titles were a popular marketing strategy at the time, which likely accounts for croquet's continental-sounding flare. Another theory is the name comes from the word *croche*, which was the term fourteenth-century French shepherds gave to the crooked sticks they used to knock wooden balls through hoops—a contest similar to croquet.

Exercise ball (Swiss ball)

In the beginning, the exercise ball was geographically confused. Invented in Italy by plastics manufacturer Aquilino Cosani, the future big ball staple in gyms around the world was originally known as the *Swiss ball*. Don't blame Cosani, who dubbed his invention the *Pezzi Gymnastik Ball* and marketed it for gymnastics in 1963. The error in location came from American students at a school in Basel, Switzerland. These budding physical therapists were taught how to integrate the ball into exercises, and when they returned to the United States, they credited Europe's neutral force for the magic ball.

Upon its arrival on American soil, the exercise ball was used to treat patients with neurological and orthopedic problems. But it didn't take long for trainers of elite athletes to realize the ball could be a valuable tool for increasing *core* strength. Basically, doing exercises while employing a large wobbly ball required work by the muscles around the gut, helping them stay healthy longer. This revelation started as early as 1986 when San Francisco 49ers quarterback Joe Montana allegedly used a Swiss ball as part of his amazing comeback from back surgery. After just six weeks of rehabilitation, Montana returned to the gridiron.

In the early 1990s, the ball made the crossover into the mainstream. One Colorado native, who was trained in Switzerland, invested $3,500 into selling Swiss balls. Within five years, she was pulling in more than $1 million in sales. Nowadays it's nearly impossible to see a TV montage of a professional athlete training without viewing one of these balls. In 2005, British newspaper the *Telegraph* credited the ball when England's cricket team won the Ashes, its highly contentious test series against Australia, for the first time in eighteen years. England's cricketers morphed into stunning athletes, claimed the *Telegraph*, in large part because of "the 'Swiss ball'—a spherical rubbery balloon that looks as if it belongs in a 1970s seating arrangement surrounded by lava lamps and inflatable armchairs."

Exercise ball mania grew so big in the mid-2000s that some began touting them for other uses. The ball has become a handy tool for pregnant women in labor. Called "birthing balls" in these situations, the big spheres are said to relieve pressure, increase relaxation, and help the baby make its way into the world. Others have argued that the balls are a fine alternative to chairs. The theory goes that the balls both work abdominal muscles and promote good posture. That rationale was good enough for many office workers throughout North America. In addition, some schools in Canada even replaced chairs with colorful balls in the classroom.

And yet some have shied away from claims that the

exercise ball has practically unlimited utility. Researchers at Canada's University of Waterloo found that sitting on a ball instead of a chair led to mixed results. They cautioned that for some back pain sufferers, the ball could lead to increased problems. The scientists also warned that developing a "numb bum" was also common.

Even worse, faulty balls have been the downfall for some athletes. In 2009, Francisco Garcia, a forward for basketball's Sacramento Kings, broke his wrist when an exercise ball popped while he was lying on the ball lifting weights. A year earlier, University of Florida basketball player Hudson Fricke broke both his wrists during a similar incident. Such examples have not deterred manufacturers. In fact, Cosani—the ball's original Italian father—continues to refine his handiwork. His company claims that a recent new durable design eliminates the potential of "sudden ball failure."

STATS AND FACTS

Dimensions: Different manufacturers recommend different-sized balls for different heights. The three typical diameters are 22 inches for smaller users (4 feet, 8 inches to 5 feet, 5 inches); 26 inches for the midrange (5 feet, 6 inches to 6 feet), and 30 inches for taller athletes (6 feet and above). A 16-inch ball is also available for kids. When inflated, weights tend to vary from about 1 to 2 pounds.

Strange But True: In 2009, a man was arrested in Duluth, Minnesota, for attempting to break into a medical building. The reason for the act, he claimed, was an uncontrollable fetish for slashing large exercise balls, the *Duluth News Tribune* reported.

Language: The exercise ball/Swiss ball has nearly as many names as its uses. Along with the above-mentioned, they include *physioball*, *gym ball*, *stability ball*, *Pilates ball*, *birth ball*, *therapy ball*, *body ball*, *gymnastic ball*, *fitness ball*, and *yoga ball*.

Field hockey ball

When it comes to the modern game of field hockey, the sport's original rule makers didn't quite comprehend the typical definition for a ball. Versions of field hockey date back to the Egyptians, and these early cultures used a whole host of different spheres. (Personal favorite: Australian aborigines played with a woody pear-like fruit from a tree they called the Dumbung.) But when a club in the Southeast London area of Blackheath began setting down a code for the sport in the 1860s, they decreed that a heavy all-rubber *cube* be used as the standard ball.

There are many reasons why cubes are not a good choice for ball sports. One obvious explanation is they don't roll. So it should come as no surprise that when the rubber cube bounced around awkwardly, smacking opposing players was as much a strategy as hitting the "ball." The overall approach was so violent that it didn't sit well with the sensibilities of some of England's Victorian middle and upper classes. As a result, a new set of rules emerged in the Southwest London suburb of Teddington beginning in 1871. Thankfully, as part of their effort to make field hockey more gentlemanly, out went the cube and in came a white-painted cricket ball. The orb's ability to roll—and the stick handling that came so much more easily with the round ball—made the game a far greater success. The Duke of Clarence, who was the eccentric (some say disturbed) son of the future King Edward VII, was an early adopter and spread the Teddington rules to Cambridge University, where he studied. Women, who had far too much sense to play a ball game with a cube, were also attracted to field hockey once a sphere was installed as the ball of choice. The sport quickly became the British Empire's first popular female outdoor team game.

Small changes to the ball have occurred along the way: The cricket ball seam was discarded for a perfectly round ball, and a more durable plastic shell eventually replaced the leather casing. When artificial turf became standard in international play, a dimpled ball (sort of a big golf ball) was introduced. It was found to move more efficiently on certain types of faux grass than the smooth ball. Still, the dimensions of the ball have remained constant over the years. One can only assume that the organizers were just relieved to have done away with the cube.

STATS AND FACTS

Dimensions: The specs are almost exactly the same as a cricket ball: 8.8125 to 9.25 inches in circumference and weighing 5.5 to 5.75 ounces.

Language: The term *hockey* likely comes from the French word *hocquet* (or *hoquet*), which refers to a shepherd's crook. *Hookey*, which is early English slang for a bent stick, may have also led to our modern word for the game.

Footbag (Hacky Sack)

The Hacky Sack is serendipity's ball. In the summer of 1972, two random regular guys, John Stalberger and Mike Marshall, unexpectedly met in Oregon City, Oregon. By chance, Stalberger was rehabilitating an injured knee at the time and was looking for ways to strengthen the joint. Marshall just so happened to have a little bag that he liked to kick around—or as he called it, "hack the sack"—that could help the healing process. After hours upon hours of keeping the sack in the air, they came to the conclusion that this could be a great commercial opportunity.

Stalberger and Marshall's first Hacky Sacks weren't really balls. They were small bags filled with various organic items such as rice and beans. The outer casing for high-end balls was usually some sort of hide—often leather or pigskin—while more casual sacks were constructed of denim. By the time Stalberger received a patent for the invention in 1976, the sack was filled with glass buttons and had the beginnings of a spherical shape—although it looked a little more like a soft miniature hockey puck.

Marshall tragically died of a heart attack in 1974, but Stalberger pressed on with their invention. The footbag, as it would eventually be generically known, earned college and high school fans, who used the sack for mellow noncompetitive games of kicking a ball around in a circle. In 1983, Wham-O, which had bought the rights to such fad-inducing products as the Frisbee, the Hula Hoop, and the SuperBall, recognized an opportunity and scooped up the Hacky Sack patent from Stalberger. Wham-O advertised the Hacky Sack not only as a fun toy but also a soccer trainer—a move that probably helped round the sack into its current ball shape.

Wham-O didn't control the market for long as competitors quickly kicked in. Knitted balls—known as *granny sacks* because they looked as if they were crocheted by Grandma—earned particular popularity. The glass buttons included in the Hacky Sack's original patent were replaced with everything from cherry pits to synthetic beads. It turned out that the glass buttons broke too quickly, leaving just a sandy substance. (Ironically, sand is a common modern filler.) Other innards today include mini–steel balls and plastic pellets. Casings are equally varied. Along with leather, vinyl, and yarn, synthetic suede is a favorite.

Although he sold the Hacky Sack patent, Stalberger still takes great pride in his role as cocreator of the footbag. In 2006, he estimated that since its invention, more than 250 million footbags have been sold. As for his chance encounter with Marshall that led to the ball's creation, Stalberger believes it wasn't luck that brought them together. "[Marshall's] death was devastating," Stalberger once said. "I got encouragement from our mutual friends for sure, but I also believe that God told me to finish what Mike and I had started."

STATS AND FACTS

Dimensions: Depending on the game, footbags can be between 1 and 2.5 inches in diameter and weigh from 0.71 to 2.47 ounces.

Shoes: Expert footbaggers consider Adidas' Rod Laver tennis shoes the sneakers of choice for hacking the sack. The World Footbag Association even offers directions on how to lace them for optimal performance. Check out: http://worldfootbag.com/shoelacing/shoelacing.html.

Sack of Friendship: Officials from a range of organizations believe Hacky Sacks are an ideal gift for détente. In 2002, the Ottawa, Ontario, police in Canada gave out rainbow-colored Hacky Sacks to protesters at a G8 conference. For years, the Belgium National Baseball team gave footbags to opposing teams before contests at major competitions. Why anybody considered the sack a good peace offering is a mystery.

Language: While dexterity is certainly needed to keep the Hacky Sack in the air, *Dexterity*, or *Dex* for short, is a term of art. It's used to describe the act of circling the bag with the leg(s) while the bag is in the air.

Football

Football may be the only sport in which the ball's development directly helped save lives. Over the course of decades, the sport's practitioners moved from using a soccer ball to various forms of *prolate spheroids* (a fancy term for an elliptical ball) and in the process shifted football from what was becoming a deadly game into a tough but survivable pastime.

The first recognized American football game took place between Rutgers and Princeton universities in 1869 and was far more soccer than gridiron. Most notably, the contest used a round ball and prohibited throwing or running with the sphere. Instead, it was all about kicking.

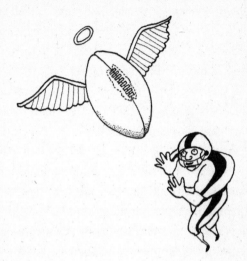

This isn't surprising because the bulky orb used would have made most modern-day football activities impossible. Not only did its circular shape make passing a dicey proposition, but the big ball also had a tendency to deflate midgame, forcing players to take turns blowing it up.

A little infusion of rugby was necessary to jolt the game—and its ball—toward its current form. For that, the high-minded folks at Harvard University paved the way. With most of their future Ivy League rivals playing their soccer-esque style, the Cambridge boys wanted something with a little more grit. After trying out rugby in a match against Canada's McGill University, they successfully persuaded Princeton, Columbia, and Yale to adopt rugby rules (with sixty-one modifications) as the basis for the American intercollegiate game. As a result, rugby's prolate spheroid became the ball for the new code in 1876.

This move to the rugby ball was far from perfect. The early spheroid "looked like a watermelon," according to a 2001 *Popular Mechanics* article, "and wasn't much easier to throw" than the soccer ball. But it did allow for laterals and short flips. By the dawn of the twentieth century, the game had morphed into a uniquely—albeit violent—American version. Offensive blocking was added as was a line of scrimmage (in contrast to rugby's scrum). These changes led to more uncontrolled contact and had coaches devising novel ways to protect the ball. The *flying wedge*, which was based on a military maneuver, was particularly effective. It featured blockers interlocking arms and practically steamrolling would-be tacklers.

These innovations could be deadly. Although sources vary on the total number of football casualties, they were definitely happening. In 1905, the *Chicago Tribune* claimed that there were eighteen college football fatalities. That year, President Teddy Roosevelt got involved. His son Theodore Jr. was a freshman player at Harvard, and after seeing him suffer minor injuries, the president took action. He summoned the coaches from Harvard, Princeton, and Yale to a meeting and suggested major changes to intercollegiate rules.

Results were not immediate. The forward pass was legalized the next year with the hope that the ability to throw downfield would de-emphasize the dangerous running game. But the bulky ball remained inadequate for hitting receivers with consistency. What was really necessary in order to make the pass a viable option was a more aerodynamic spheroid. So, in 1912, along with further liberalizing passing rules, the fathers of the game decided to dump the watermelon and went with a somewhat slimmed-down football. Forward-thinking coaches saw this move as a big opportunity. Notre Dame football legend Knute Rockne helped design a new ball in 1924 that produced the type of tight spiral that encouraged quarterbacks to go long. By the mid-1930s, the iconic prolate spheroid's dimensions were set to specifications nearly identical to today's footballs. These balls and the passing game that opened up contributed mightily to preventing fatalities.

By 1941, the National Football League was so proud of its lifesaver that it gave the spheroid a regal name: *The Duke* (after Wellington Mara, the son of the New York Giants' owner, whose first name paid homage to the Duke of Wellington). Despite its early success, the royal ball's reign ran into trouble in 1967. That year, the American Football League and the NFL competed in the first Super Bowl. The Duke came under attack from the AFL as the upstart league used a slightly different ball. Instead of the NFL's grippable leather, the AFL's ball had a sprayed-on sticky substance. The AFL ball also had longer laces, and, most important, it was sleeker and pointier than the rounder NFL style.

This last point led Vince Lombardi, the heralded coach of the NFL's Green Bay Packers, to quip before Super Bowl II that the AFL ball "looks like a Long Island frankfurter." For the first four Super Bowls the two sides compromised: Each team used their league's respective balls on offense. (It's unclear which ball offered an advantage as the NFL and AFL split the first four championship games.) When the two leagues merged after Super Bowl IV, the NFL's ball won out.

While the modern ball can fly through the air with the greatest of ease, there is a group of NFL players who have been left grumbling by its projectile-ability. For kickers, the more aerodynamic spheroid has meant fewer of the round qualities perfect for booting the ball. For years, kickers were okay with this issue because they would simply take balls and doctor them. This included baking them in aluminum foil, giving them steam baths, dunking them in water, and smacking them with hammers. The purpose: to make the ball pliable in order to shape it to suit the kicker's needs. As a result, when it came time to kick the ball through the uprights or punt it away to the opposition, the player would just bring his nicely rounded ball onto the field to do his business.

But in 1999, it all changed. The NFL mandated that twelve game balls (eight in domed stadiums) be branded with the letter *K* and be exclusively used for the kicking game. Initially, officials would get these *K Balls* about 2.5 hours before kickoff, leaving little time for tampering. For years, kickers felt that the new rules, which caused them to kick with balls that were not broken in, hurt their game. In 2006, kickers and punters caught a break when a high-profile flub gave them a chance to press their issue anew. In the play-offs, the Dallas Cowboys' Tony Romo dropped a snap for a placekick that cost his team a game. Some suggested that a slippery K Ball was the reason for the miscue. Now, rules provide each team 45 minutes to "prepare" K Balls prior to games. Despite this allowance, the NFL still takes the K Ball seriously. An extra official called a K Ball coordinator is hired at every stadium to keep track of the balls during games and make sure the spheroids don't end up too round. After all, the pointy ball did save lives.

STATS AND FACTS

Dimensions: The ball is 11 to 11.5 inches long, its tip-to-tip circumference is 28 to 28.5 inches, and its circumference around the middle is 20.75 to 21.25 inches. The ball weighs between 14 and 15 ounces.

Pigskin: From the beginning, the balls' outer shells were made of cowhide. Calling the ball *the pigskin* related to the prerubber days when pig bladders were used inside these first balls.

Grip: Though laces are no longer needed for access to the ball's bladder, they remain because they've proved important for grip. The laces—eight of them crossing over a central lace—are made of a durable substance known as grid cord.

Strange But True: In the nineteenth century, scoring reflected the game's early emphasis on kicking. The 1883 rules awarded a field goal 5 points and the kick after a touchdown 4 points. A touchdown resulted in a meager 2 points.

Language: The *ogive* (pronounced *oh-jive*) is the term used for the football's arch from the laces to the nose of the ball. In the late 1960s, the NFL's ball had a more rounded ogive than the AFL's version, causing controversy.

Gaelic football

The battle of the balls. That's how prominent Irish sports historian Eoghan Corry described the formative years of Gaelic football in his 2009 book *The History of Gaelic Football*. Like Australian Rules football (see page 1), Gaelic football developed in the late 1800s as a hybrid between the emerging sports of soccer and rugby. But unlike the Aussies, who grappled with what shape of ball to use in their code, the Irish seem to have been certain from the start—only a round ball would do. In fact, there must have been enough certainty about going spherical (rather than elliptical) that the original rules, first published in 1885, didn't even offer any specifications for the ball.

So what was the conflict about? In the final decades of the nineteenth century, the clash was over which sport would win the hearts and minds of Irish folk—the emerging Gaelic football or the British-born rugby. Would it be the orb or the oval that would reign supreme? The short answer is Irish pride would not be denied. Founded in 1885, the Gaelic Athletic Association (GAA) made protecting the round ball sport a priority. This effort hit critical mass in 1902, when the GAA decreed a ban on foreign sports. The rule excommunicated any member of the GAA caught playing or supporting non-Irish games— most notably the British sports of rugby, soccer, and cricket. There were no exceptions: One important patron was kicked out because he went to an international soccer game, and a prominent athlete got expelled after attending a dance sponsored by a soccer club.

The draconian measures, which stayed on the books

until 1971, did the trick. Gaelic football, which is a rough game mixing elements similar to soccer (there are netted goals) and rugby (the ball can be carried), became a wildly popular spectator sport throughout Ireland. Still, settling on uniform characteristics for the ball didn't happen immediately. As early as 1886, a Dublin sporting goods store was offering up unique Gaelic footballs alongside soccer and rugby balls. But the footballs must have varied greatly as it was customary in the early days for each team to provide its own ball for one half of the match.

While not rugby shaped, early balls were heavy and not completely round. They could also be really big. An 1887 photo of a Limerick team shows a ball about the diameter of a small beach ball. Whatever the size, the leather balls would inevitably get soaked and misshapen on the wet Irish turf. Players devised a new style of passing the ball along the ground to overcome this soggy problem. (This type of passing was later outlawed after water-resistant coating was added to the ball.)

The GAA eventually hooked up with an exclusive supplier for the balls, and a universal size—about the same as a basketball with a paneled design like a volleyball—became the norm.

STATS AND FACTS

Dimensions: It's approximately 10 inches in diameter and weighs roughly 13 to 15 ounces.

Strange But True: In 1947, the GAA transported the All-Ireland Gaelic football finals to the United States. With New York's large Irish population, the organization figured they could fill one of baseball's hallowed stadiums, the Polo Grounds, with Gaelic football fans. While some were disappointed with the attendance, approximately 35,000 came out to watch Cavan beat Kerry.

Language: The sport of Gaelic football is often known by the shorthand name *Gah*.

Golf ball

For those who want to give thanks for golf, be sure to offer praise to the Hindu deity Vishnu. The all-pervading god deserves credit for helping propel golf balls toward their modern form. Alas, much to the chagrin of duffers in Scotland, where the game grew up, it took centuries

before Vishnu's intervention. At first the Scots knocked around hardwood—usually boxwood—balls. They rarely traveled more than 100 yards so craftsmen came up with a little orb in the fifteenth century known as a *feathery*.

Slightly smaller than the modern ball, the feathery could fly twice as far as the wooden version, but required serious hardship to produce. Little leather strips were soaked in alum, hand-sewn, and then stuffed with boiled feathers (typically goose). An artisan would cram the equivalent of a top hat full of feathers into the orbs using a long metal rod known as a *brogue*. The stitched ball, which grew hard as the wet leather shrank and the feathers expanded, was then treated with oil to add some water resistance. The painstaking process meant that only four or five balls could be completed in a day. It was also tough on the ball makers, who tended to develop asthma and die young as result of inhaling the feathers and suffering from injuries sustained from pushing the brogue against their chest while filling balls.

With all the effort involved, these balls were not cheap. At one point, the cost was probably higher than necessary as a single man held a monopoly on the Scottish production for part of the feathery's time in the spotlight. In 1618, James Melvill successfully petitioned King James for the sole right to construct golf balls. Melvill wasn't actually a *ball stuffer*, as they were known in some parts, but thanks to the king, any artisan who wanted to enter the trade had to first get a license from Melvill. While the monopoly lasted only twenty-one years, it surely contributed to a feathery costing twelve times as much as its wooden predecessors. With such an exorbitant price tag, the sport of golf was generally limited to the upper classes.

Then Vishnu arrived in 1843. Well, actually, it was a statue of the Hindu god that was delivered to the Scottish home of St. Andrews University professor Dr. Robert Paterson that made the difference. The likeness of Vishnu was transported in an old-school version of packing peanuts—shavings of a soft gum from the Malaysian sapodilla tree. Dr. Paterson kept the rubbery substance known as *gutta percha* because he found it could be melted down to resole shoes.

As the Paterson family lived in St. Andrews, the cradle of modern golf, it's not surprising that the good doctor's son, Robert Adam Paterson, was an avid—albeit frustrated—golfer. The problem: The divinity student was frustrated because he couldn't afford the pricey featheries. Seeing the gutta percha in action, the young Paterson began forming the material into golf balls. His invention, dubbed the *gutty*, wasn't perfect. It would split (players were allowed to drop a new ball where the biggest piece of the splintered sphere sat), and it didn't necessarily fly farther than the feathery. But the gutty was more weather resistant than its forerunner and, most important, was far less expensive. Mass-produced in a way impossible with the feathery, it could be purchased for four to five times less than the stuffed ball.

Vishnu's gift took about two decades to fully replace the feathery. Quite quickly, the new ball spurred loads of development. Players found that bumps in a bramble pattern on the gutty's outer casing helped the ball travel farther. Gutty composites, containing a combination of the gummy substance with a host of other materials such as ground cork and metal fillings, improved the durability and playability of the ball.

Although the gutty revolutionized the game by making golf balls more financially accessible, the combination of increased mechanization and the discovery of vulcanization (the industrial ability to shape rubber) meant it would have a short reign as the ruler of the links. Not surprisingly, the Goodyear Rubber Co. was at the center of the next ball breakthrough. Known as *Bounding Billy* (golfers sure like their nicknames), this sphere was developed in large part by some Goodyear employees and featured machine-wrapped rubber threads wound tightly around a gutta percha core. The invention, which came to market around 1900, lived up to its name as it flew between 20 and 50 yards longer than the gutty. It also bounced with aplomb across the ground. The high-flying ball required courses to be lengthened and golf clubs to be redesigned. "Without question the most significant change in golf equipment...was the development of the wound ball," famed golfer Bobby Jones once concluded.

Since then, the golf ball has enjoyed a steady march toward the finely tuned explosive balls we see today. A. G. Spalding, a sporting goods mogul who had his tentacles in nearly every ball sport, popularized many different designs in the first half of the twentieth century. His most long-lasting change was the outer covering's dimple design. Patented by a British engineer in 1908, dimples immediately became a staple for Spalding balls, and other companies followed, competing for the most aerodynamic pattern.

Although golf potentates first set weight and diameter standards in 1920 (they would be changed over the years), companies came up with new ways to meet the criteria. Scientists became experts at manipulating the elements of the core and shell to change the ball's distance, loft, spin, feel, control, and durability. Emblematic of the high-tech charge, Titleist, which would become a world leader in golf balls, was founded in the 1930s by M.I.T. graduates. As if speaking for an industry, Titleist explained in a 1999 ad for a new ball: "You don't need a PhD in astrophysics to appreciate Titleist HP2. (But it wouldn't hurt.)" It seems that when it comes to the links, science has now supplanted the mystic power of Vishnu.

STATS AND FACTS

Dimensions: A standard tournament ball is 1.68 inches in diameter and weighs 1.62 ounces.

Name Game: Most scholars believe the term *golf* comes from an old Teutonic word meaning "club."

Variation: The United States Golf Association recognizes more than 1,000 different balls that conform to the organization's basic standards.

Strange But True: In the early 1680s, the Duke of York, who would later become King James II, spent a couple of years as the King's Lord High Commissioner in Scotland. He was once challenged to a golf game for which he would have to find a partner. The duke heard a poor shoemaker named John Patersone was quite good so he asked the commoner to join him. Patersone played well, and the prince and the local cobbler won. The duke was so pleased that he gave Patersone half the winnings wagered on the match. (Far more money than the lowly shoemaker had probably ever seen.) The sensible Patersone used the money to build a house on one of Edinburgh's finest streets, and the future king had a special coat of arms made for the front of the house that featured a golf club and the motto "Far and Sure."

Taking Aim: The diameter of a golf hole is 4.25 inches. It was set in 1898.

Language: In 1899, the term *bird* was a popular word used to describe a top achievement in the United States. During a golf game in Atlantic City, New Jersey, that year, a player named Abner Smith described a particularly success pitch as a "bird of a shot." From that statement, a *birdie* became the term for holing a ball one under par. A particularly impressive bird—an *eagle*—was used for two shots under par.

Handball

Seeking a simple definition of a handball is like being asked to answer yes or no when only an essay will do. Sure, you could say that it's a sphere with some bounce that's slapped against a wall, but that tells you almost nothing about the multitude of balls used in this sport. Whether you're in the United States, Mexico, Ireland, Spain, France, England (I could go on, but I think you get the picture), the ball, the rules, and the name of what is essentially handball will be vastly different.

Games that feature smacking a small ball by hand date back to the Egyptians. Mesoamericans, who were the first to figure out how to turn rubber into a sphere, separately developed their own handball sports. Europeans were introduced to these types of games by Alexander the Great when he colonized Italy. In France, there was eventually *jeu de paume* (which was really a handball forerunner to tennis), and in Scotland, there was *caich*. Even the philosopher Erasmus supported an early form of handball when he commented in his 1527 *Colloquies* that playing with the hand was more elegant than handling a racquet.

Playing off a wall or multiple walls became an increasingly popular style of hand play by the sixteenth century. Over the next few centuries, every European country seemed to have its own versions. The Spanish played *Valencia pilota* or *Basque pelota*, the Italians had *pallone* and *pallapugno*, the British played *fives*, and the Irish had *handball*. In the New World, Mexico enjoyed *pelota mixteca*, and the Americans took bits of the Irish game and created their own type of handball. Of course, each of these games had their own ball. In fact, within each of these sports, there are subdisciplines that require spheres of different sizes and weights.

For most Americans, a rubber racquetball-esque projectile is probably the most recognizable. This is the ball that fit, leathery old men use in the parks of New York. Head indoors and you'll find the game being played with a smaller, harder ball. (The Irish use similar orbs.) In Spain, a number of different spheres are in play, ranging from the golf ball–sized *vaqueta ball*, which is made of bull leather, to the softball-sized ball constructed of cloth and plaster used in *galotxetes*. The ball in pallapugno appears similar in diameter to the one used in galotxetes, but the Italians' version is inflated and lighter. Keeping with history, Mexicans use a rubber ball for pelota mixteca—although modern versions have some synthetic materials and are larger than the small balls used ages ago. As for the British, size and consistency depend on the fancy boarding school where you learned the game. At Eton, a posh institution located near Windsor where eighteen different prime ministers were educated, their modern fives ball is made of a rubber and cork composite. At Rugby, situated in England's West Midlands region, the ball's core is formed by cork soaked in liquid rubber and its seams glued. Hampshire's Winchester (yet another high-end school) has its own variation.

Confused yet? Even handball experts are probably befuddled by all the ball options available. There have been efforts to harmonize the games, but it's been an ongoing struggle. Clearly, either a simple yes or no won't do when it comes to handball.

STATS AND FACTS

Dimensions: As discussed, it's impossible to give a size for the typical handball. But the one most often seen in the United States is 1.875 inches in diameter (with a 0.03125-inch variation). It weighs 2.3 ounces (give or take 0.2 ounce).

Strange But True: Along with all the knobs, flashing lights, and levers in the first-ever American human-piloted spacecraft was a sign that warned: "No Handball Playing Here." The placard was placed in the *Freedom 7* capsule by John Glenn as a joke for pilot Alan Shepard. The reason: Handball had been part of the astronauts' training regime.

Language: In New York, a shot that hits where the wall and the floor meet is called a *crotch ball*.

Jai alai pelota

Forget the baseball. Sport's true hardball is the jai alai pelota.

For those of you who missed out on the opening credits to *Miami Vice* back in the 1980s, jai alai (pronounced

"HIGH-lie") is a sport with rules similar to racquetball or squash. Each competing player uses a curved wicker basket called a *cesta* attached to his right arm to take turns throwing the pelota (ball) in a three-wall court. The leverage created by the cesta hurtles the pelota at dizzying speeds. The current record for a throw is 188 miles per hour and shots of more than 150 miles per hour are typical.

The ball is literally one of a kind. Jai alai is one—if not the only—current professional sport in the world in which every ball is handmade. No two bounce or move the same way. The core of the pelota is constructed of tightly wound layers of Brazilian virgin *de pola* rubber. That center is then wrapped in a nylon thread and finally covered in *two* outer shells of tough goatskin (in the past it was the same type of hide used to cover drum heads and banjos). The result is a ball about three-fourths the size of a baseball but harder than a golf ball.

How hard is it? The front wall, which gets the brunt of the pelota's power, is traditionally made of granite because concrete is too easily dented by the speeding projectile. Granite may allow the wall to retain its integrity, but the ball isn't as lucky. A pelota will last about 15 to 20 minutes before its top goat cover begins to fray and the ball becomes unusable. Every jai alai arena has a resident ball maker who not only fashions new pelotas but also spends hours fixing used balls. After each game day, a ball maker can find himself unraveling approximately twenty knocked-out-of-shape pelotas and reweaving them. With the tender care of the ball maker, a pelota can last for years, but the price tag for constructing and fixing each ball has been estimated at between $100 and $200— and that's not including labor costs.

Dubbed by one newspaper as "the most lethal ball used in sports," it's not quite clear how many people have met their maker thanks to a whirling pelota. In the sport's American heyday, a 1962 *Miami Herald* article vaguely put the total at eight "in recent years." The report did not indicate where these deaths took place, but with helmets becoming mandatory in 1968 in Florida, which is the game's most popular American locale, injuries such as broken bones seem to be more likely than death for U.S. players.

In the sport's homeland of Spain, this might not be the case. The game was invented in the Spanish-French Basque region and has been described there as "the game of dodging death." The sport, known as *cesta punta* in Spanish, developed from handball. One legend suggests that the cesta was introduced in the nineteenth century when a player grabbed his mother's wicker basket and used it in a handball game. Through its Spanish connections, cesta punta spread to Cuba and elsewhere in the Americas. It eventually landed in the United States as an exhibition at the 1904 World's Fair in Saint Louis. (The name *jai alai*, which means "merry festival" in Basque, was coined as a way to market it at the fair.) In 1934, Florida legalized wagering on contests and the sport flourished for decades with a record 15,502 spectators attending a Miami jai alai session on December 27, 1975.

Yet over the years, the sport has lost ground to slot machines and casinos, leaving jai alai's future—and the prospects for master ball makers—in the United States in question. At least there is a sense of humor about the situation among some in the industry. Contemplating the end of his profession, Florida pelota maker Jose "Paco" Gonzalez discussed the topic with the *Fort Lauderdale Sun-Sentinel* newspaper in 2008. "I'll learn how to deal cards," he deadpanned.

STATS AND FACTS

Dimensions: The pelota is between 2 and 2.5 inches in diameter and weighs approximately 4.5 ounces.

Quick Action: The average game lasts about 13 minutes.

Language: Jai alai arenas are called *frotons*. The court (or *cancha*) consists of three walls and ranges in size (176 feet long and 50 feet wide are popular dimensions). The front wall is called the *frontis* and is 40 feet high. The side wall is named the *lateral*, and the back wall the *rebote*.

OUTLAW BALLS

The law has not always been kind to balls. History is full of examples of great (and not so great) leaders banning the use of balls. One estimate puts the number of soccer bans over the years at more than thirty in England alone. Below is a sampling of some of those dark moments:

1314: England's Edward II banned football (aka soccer). According to the proclamation: "Forasmuch as there is great noise in the city caused by hustling over large balls from which many evils might arise which God forbid: we command and forbid on behalf of the King, on pain of imprisonment, such to be used in the city in future."

1365: Edward III outlawed a number of ball games in England including "casting the stone" (aka shot put) and "bandy-ball"—the forerunner to both modern bandy ball and field hockey.

1369: France's Charles VI prohibited an early ball sport called *la soule*.

1427: "Futeball" (aka soccer) was outlawed in Scotland. This is just one of many ball bans in Scotland (others occurred in 1457, 1471, and 1491).

1576: The Republic of Venice stopped the sport of bocce. Players caught enjoying the game were fined and imprisoned.

1835: The British Highways Act prohibited playing soccer on public highways.

1898: Lawn bowling was banned in Boston thanks to heavy gambling (and drinking) that occurred during matches.

continues . . .

. . . continued from previous page

1934: Los Angeles prohibited the use of pinball machines based on concerns that it is merely a wagering game of chance. (A number of other municipalities, including New York, had similar bans.)

Before 1988: Paintball was outlawed in New Jersey because the game's guns were considered to be firearms. The game was legalized in the state on May 2, 1988.

2009: Rio de Janeiro banned the soccer ball–based game of *altinho* (also known by Brazilians as *keepie uppie*) on its 54 miles of local beaches. The purpose was to bring order to the area and help women and kids avoid getting hit by balls on the way to the ocean.

Ki

Some balls are uniquely emblematic of a culture. The *ki* is one such example. For New Zealand's Māori people, the ki, which means "ball" in their language, is woven from plants indigenous to New Zealand and has been used in the country since they arrived more than 1,000 years ago.

Playing ball has always been a serious event for the Māori. The games enjoyed by these first nation people had great religious importance with the sphere often representing the all-sustaining sun. While the size of the ki varied greatly, New Zealand flax or other forms of local vegetation like *kuka* were used to make it. The ball usually included a braided strapping, which had two roles. Along with being a handy grip at game time, the strap

could also be unwound, turning the ki into a warrior training device known as a *poi-toa* or *warrior poi*. (This ball on a rope would be thrown at soldiers during military training in order to test agility, quickness, and flexibility.) Even today, crafting a ki is considered a special event and a first-time maker customarily presents his or her initial creation as a gift to a family member or special individual.

With each tribe sporting its own rules, the ki games historically had different names such as *haka*, *riki*, *rahi*, *kiarahi*, and *tapawai*, but since World War II they have consolidated into a single title: *ki-o-rahi* (meaning "ball raise up the sun"). Despite its significance in Māori culture (or probably because of it), early European settlers looked to stanch tribal games. In the 1870s, they took away the local spheres and replaced them with rugby balls. As the Māori ki sports had a lot of similarity to the English's highly physical rugby, the locals excelled at the foreign game. Still, efforts were made to resist this Westernization. For example, Princess Te Puea pushed for the Māori to return to traditional ki games during World War I.

After a long political scrum, ki-o-rahi was finally recognized as a national game of New Zealand in the 1970s. The fast-moving contact sport played on a circular field has enjoyed somewhat of a resurgence in recent years. Unfortunately, modern times have meant that the ki is now often replaced by a team handball.

STATS AND FACTS

Dimensions: Ball sizes generally vary from 6 to 10 inches in diameter, with the majority of ki coming in at between 6 and 7 inches. The weight can range from a couple of ounces to 2 pounds.

Ki-o-Rahi in America: In 2005, McDonald's chose ki-o-rahi as part of a program to teach fifteen different ethnic games to some 31,000 elementary schools in the United States. It was said at the time that this would lead to more people playing ki-o-rahi in America than in its native New Zealand.

Language: The word *ki* is both the singular and the plural for a ball. "The context gives the clue to the numbers," according to Harko Brown, author of the book *Nga Taonga Takaro: Maori Sports and Games.* "For example, my nana made several ki [plural] or I couldn't find the ki so I made another [singular]."

Koosh Ball

The patent for the Koosh Ball described it clinically as "an amusement device which has a substantially spherical configuration . . . formed from a large plurality of floppy, elastomeric filaments that radiate in a dense, bushy manner from a central core region." Thankfully for its inventors, the public saw it, according to one observer, as more of "a cross between Jell-O and a porcupine."

A frizzy creation of between 2,000 and 5,000 brightly colored strands of latex rubber, the Koosh was the brainchild of a design engineer named Scott Stillinger, who was having trouble teaching his two children how to play catch. A normal ball would pop right out of his five- and eight-year-olds' hands so he pondered a way to produce an easy-to-handle sphere that would have no bounce and could be pain-free to catch. "I intuitively knew that a rubber-filament ball would do the trick," he recalled a few years later. His prototype was energy absorbent (hence, no bouncing away from the kids), lightweight, tickly, and malleable. Pleased with his efforts, Stillinger showed it to Mark Button, his brother-in-law, who had previously worked in marketing at Mattel Inc.

Button was so convinced it was a winner that he and Stillinger quit their jobs and set up a toy company selling the balls. At first, there was reason for concern. The media reveled in poking fun at the soft ball. A *Sports Illustrated* writer compared the Koosh to a Star Trek tribble, while another reporter likened it to a "psychedelic sea urchin." More worrying, some industry veterans didn't know what to make of the ball. At an early showing, a representative for a potential retailer started cutting bits off the Koosh, believing the tendrils were a defect.

But shoppers didn't make the same mistake. Beginning Christmas 1988, the balls became a top seller in the toy world. Stillinger and Button didn't rest on the one design, concocting other ways to repackage their ball, including a larger version called the Mondo Koosh and key chains. In a true sign that the ball had novelty appeal, Archie Comics produced a 1991 *Koosh Kins* comic book about a group of six living Kooshes (complete with toy tie-in). Needless to say, it lasted only a few issues.

Maybe because they understood the life cycle of what has been described as an "impulse buy" or maybe it was for other reasons, but Stillinger and Button sold their Koosh Ball company in 1994. Knockoffs were becoming rampant by that point. A 1991 court decision by Judge Ruth Bader Ginsburg—in her pre–Supreme Court days—refusing to recognize a copyright for the Koosh Ball helped alternative brands. Nevertheless, at the time of the sale, the company had sold 50 million balls and boasted $30 million in annual revenues. The Koosh Ball would be passed along again in 1997, when Hasbro Inc. bought it as part of a $166 million deal.

After Stillinger and Button departed, the ball continued to show surprising resiliency in the marketplace. Comedian Rosie O'Donnell made flinging Koosh Balls into her audience a staple on her talk show, which aired from 1996 to 2002. (Alas, an elderly lady did sue the program after being hit in the face with a Koosh during a 2001 taping.) The Koosh also became popular as a therapy tool for kids dealing with a variety of disorders from autism to dyslexia.

In 2010, a business called Basic Fun licensed the right to sell the Koosh from Hasbro. The company's pitch: "This combination of texture, sound and color makes Koosh a timeless toy and irresistible plaything for kids of all ages."

STATS AND FACTS

Dimensions: The classic Koosh is approximately 3 inches in diameter and weighs 1.7 ounces.

The Name: Stillinger and Button decided on the Koosh moniker after careful testing. They brainstormed more than 200 candidate names before settling on a list of finalists. They then asked a group of kids and adults to pick their favorite. It was "a process of surveys and logic," Stillinger said. Licensee Basic Fun says the name is inspired by the sound the ball makes when caught.

Games: *The Official Koosh Book*, which was first published in 1989, offered up thirty-three different games featuring the Koosh Ball, including such oddly named crowd pleasers as "Bop the Brother" and "Koosh Squoosh."

Language: *Feelers* was the slightly creepy title the inventors gave to the Koosh Ball's tentacles.

Lacrosse ball

Some Native Americans who first played lacrosse thought of it as "The Creator's Game"—a sport designed for the amusement of the heavens. When it came to the ball, the Almighty was pretty flexible.

More than four dozen tribes throughout North America enjoyed variations of lacrosse. It was often used as an exercise in preparing for battle—or even, on occasion,

in lieu of an actual tussle between warring tribes. Some also believed that the game had spiritual qualities, with a good lacrosse match preserving the well-being of a community (hence, possibly, the divine interest). The contests featured different projectiles depending on the rules particular to the region and the materials available. Certain clans played with knots of wood (the Chippewa used the same word for "play ball" and "knob of a tree"). Others like the Mohawk and the Choctaw went with a lighter deerskin ball, stuffed with animal hair. The Dakota would sometimes use a clay ball covered with hide, which was said to possess supernatural powers. There are stories that, in some tribes, a member of the losing team would be sacrificed and his head used as a ball. If true, this does not appear to be the norm.

When Europeans got their hands on the sport, they

took religion out of the game. A Montreal resident named W. George Beers was the point man for the Westernization of lacrosse and, regrettably, to some extent, did so under the racist guise of civilizing the sport. (He once wrote that the "white" version of lacrosse was superior to the traditional form like "a pretty Canadian girl is to any uncultivated squaw.") A priority for Beers was creating a new ball. In place of the handmade options, he insisted on a vulcanized India rubber sphere slightly smaller than a baseball. For Beers, the ball was the centerpiece for what he believed was an improved game. Lacrosse "unbends the mind better than any other sport because of the ubiquity of the ball," Beers cryptically wrote in his 1869 book *Lacrosse: The National Game of Canada.*

One can only assume that Beers was a better salesman than a writer because lacrosse did take off in Canada. For much of the mid- to late nineteenth century it was the country's most popular sport and its ubiquity (as Beers might put it) actually contributed to its ultimate downfall as Canada's favored game. Ice hockey was developing around the time lacrosse got big. Originally a ball was used, but it was pretty unwieldy on the ice. Circular wooden blocks were an alternative but weren't great. Then in 1886, students from Queen's University and cadets from the Royal Military College figured a lacrosse ball could be the answer. Before a game in Kingston, Ontario, they cut off either side of a ball to produce a flat disk and, voilà, the hockey puck was born. Ice hockey was never the same and lacrosse receded as a loved, but decidedly second-tier, sport in Canada.

STATS AND FACTS

Dimensions: The ball has a 7.75- to 8-inch circumference and weighs between 5 and 5.25 ounces.

Colors: Orange, white, yellow, and lime green are used depending on the league.

Spring: Lacrosse balls are surprisingly full of hop. A regulation ball must bounce between 45 and 49 inches when dropped from a height of 72 inches.

Language: When first seeing the sport, French settlers were said to have described the instrument used for throwing the ball as a *crosse*—a term for a curved stick. This supposedly evolved into *lacrosse* and stuck as the game's name. Native Americans had a variety of titles for the sport. The Mohawk called it *tewaarathon* (meaning "little brother of war"); the Onondaga referred to it as *dehuntshigwa'es* ("men hit a rounded object"); the Eastern Cherokee dubbed it *da-nah-wah'uwsdi* ("little war"); and the Chippewa named it *baggataway* ("they bump hips").

Lawn bowling balls (bowls/woods)

The English-speaking world's version of *bocce* (see page 34)—complete with different rules and strategies—may have been the result of a broken ball. As the story goes, in 1522, Charles Brandon, who was the Duke of Suffolk, was in the midst of a heated bocce-esque game when his ball split. Keen to finish the match, he retired briefly to his palace, sawed off the round top of an ornamental banister, and came back to complete the contest. The

spot where the ball was sawed was flat, leaving the newly shaped *bowl* lopsided. The creation would no longer roll straight but would curve at the end of its roll—an action dubbed *bias*. As the duke was Henry VIII's brother-in-law, it would seem unlikely that anybody would question this new off-kilter orb. This led to the game of *bowls* (known as *lawn bowling* in the United States), which is quite different from the straight-shooting bocce.

Then again, the duke's story might be wholly apocryphal and the real truth of how Britain got its bowls curving has been lost in the mists of time. This wouldn't be surprising because, while lawn bowling today may conjure images of the geriatric set decked out in their best

Sunday whites, centuries ago it was grist for tall tales and loose morals.

Beginning in the late thirteenth century, the British enjoyed the art of rolling balls on manicured lawns. Spheres in these early days were made of ash, yew, and other woods common in the British Isles, leading to the term *woods* for the balls. But as the duke's unfortunate loss illustrated, these indigenous materials would easily come apart over time.

Much to the joy of the sporting men and women of Britain, one by-product of imperialism was the discovery of a wood that could hold up. In the 1500s, *lignum vitae* was brought back from the New World. The hardest of all traded woods, lignum vitae also boasted a very high resin content, making it extremely watertight. The result was a perfect material for fashioning these larger-than-softball-sized bowls.

Though it's unclear which balls he was using, Sir Francis Drake's penchant for playing the woods is at the center of one of England's most popular legends. On July 19, 1588, the famed sea captain was in the midst of a tight contest with fellow captain Sir John Hawkins on Plymouth Hoe close to the British shores when he was informed that the Spanish Armada was sighted off the English coast. It's said that Drake contemplated the situation and replied that he had time to finish the contest before engaging with the enemy. Drake lost the bowls contest but went on to defeat the Spanish in what would be one of his country's most famous and important naval battles. While most historians dismiss the story as a myth, some cling tightly to it.

Unfortunately for its fairer participants, bowls also became the sport for all the wrong elements. Wrote one author: "A Bowling-green . . . is a place where three things are thrown away besides the Bowls . . . Time, Money and Curses, and the last ten for one." Wagering on matches was rampant, leading to numerous nationwide bans on the sport. As one would expect, allowances were made for landowners and nobility. This was necessary as bowls was a passion for many kings. In fact, Charles I was known to place £1,000 wagers on matches, which was an exorbitant sum for the seventeenth century. His son, Charles II, penned the first formal rules for the game with the Duke of York and the Duke of Buckingham in 1670.

The king's code (later updated by a Scottish lawyer named William W. Mitchell) was essential as the Duke of Suffolk's supposed invention of curving balls led to tremendous variations in rules throughout England. Some games would allow for a ball with just a little swing while others had woods that could perform a full semicircle. With wagering involved, the ground rules on the balls were definitely a critical factor.

Today, machine-made balls—wood was replaced by synthetic or composite plastic resin balls in the 1930s— are clearly stamped with information about the bowls' bias. Players do have leeway and can choose from a range of different curving balls. The bowls also have markings to indicate which side is heavier (that's the side on which the ball will curve). Still, it's not unheard of for a bowler to deliver a *wrong bias* shot and have the wood curve in an unexpected direction. Unlike the days of the Duke of

Suffolk, you can't just search for the marks where the ball was sawed off a banister.

STATS AND FACTS

Dimensions: Bowls range from 4.5 to 5.125 inches in diameter. They weigh between 2.5 and 3.5 pounds. The *jack*, which is the ball the bowlers aim for, is a maximum diameter of 2.5 inches and weighs 10 ounces.

Bowls in the United States: The sport allegedly had some high-profile early supporters, including George Washington. The Revolutionary War soured many on what was perceived as a British game, but the sport had a comeback in the nineteenth century, eventually luring such luminaries as Walt Disney and George Vanderbilt.

Shakespeare: Though William Shakespeare's references can sometimes be veiled, one author put the number of the Bard's works with mentions of bowls at ten. They are *Love's Labours Lost*, *Richard II*, *The Tempest*, *Coriolanus*, *Timon of Athens*, *The Merry Wives of Windsor*, *The Taming of the Shrew*, *Twelfth Night*, *The Winter's Tale*, and *Cymbeline*.

Language: Many scholars give bowls enthusiasts credit for inventing the sporting phrase *a rubber match*, which sportscasters use to describe the deciding contest in a three-game (or longer) series between two teams. Beginning in the late sixteenth century, the deciding game in a bowls match was called *the rubber*.

Magic 8 Ball

Will this section be interesting?
BETTER NOT TO TELL YOU NOW.

The Magic 8 Ball is wisely waiting for more information before answering that one. No doubt, the Magic 8 Ball is one of the ball world's strangest entries. After all, why should we trust an answer-spewing sphere in the shape of a billiard ball? (REPLY HAZY, TRY AGAIN LATER.) Well, the first thing to note is that this fortune teller wasn't originally an orb and it came from a person who possessed legitimate occult roots. Was this good news for would-be sports gamblers who might rely on this ball? DON'T COUNT ON IT.

Albert Carter was the son of a Cincinnati clairvoyant who had been successful enough to offer information on the "other side" to the likes of Sir Arthur Conan Doyle, author of the Sherlock Holmes books. Al was a boozer and a regular at flophouses, but had a canny mechanical sense (maybe he knew something we didn't). In 1944, he filed a patent application for a "liquid dice agitator." It was a cylinder filled with a "heavy viscous liquid" and had a pair of dice—one on either side of a central barrier. When the tube was turned in one direction one of the die would float to the top with an answer, and when turned the other way, the other cube would be summoned to the surface. Along with some local businessmen, Carter, who would pass away not long after his invention, began selling the *Syco-Seer*, a 7-inch-long cylinder marketed as "The Miracle Home Fortune Teller."

Was the new device a runaway success? MY SOURCES SAY NO. Despite a fascination in the hereafter during this period, the *Syco-Seer* and another version called the *Syco-Slate*, which had only a single answer-giving die, weren't huge money spinners. What it needed was a rounder shape (OUTLOOK GOOD). In 1948, Alabe Crafts, which owned Carter's original patent, took the liquid dice agitator cylinder and stuck it in a crystal-ball-looking sphere. It really took off after Brunswick Billiards commissioned a set of the spheres in the form of 8 balls for a promotion in 1950, according to author and toy expert Tim Walsh. Has it been a steady seller since? IT IS CERTAIN.

STATS AND FACTS

Dimensions: Approximately 4 inches in diameter and weighs 11.2 ounces.

Icosahedron: That's the fancy way of saying that rather than a cube inside the Magic 8 Ball, a twenty-sided die is used. The icosahedron is hollow, which makes it easier to drift to the top. To keep things positive, ten of the possible answers on the icosahedron are affirmative, five are negative, and five are noncommittal (such as ASK AGAIN LATER).

Viscous Liquid: For most of the 8 Ball's existence, the oozy stuff used to hold the twenty-sided die has been a combination of alcohol and blue dye.

Strange But True: In the early years of the Magic 8 Ball, residents of one city—Washington, DC—bought a disproportionate number of the fortune-telling balls. In 1958, Magic 8 Ball sales manager Sidney Korey told the

New York Times that denizens of the nation's capital would write in because "they want[ed] to know if the answers are accurate. They want[ed] to know if they can depend on the 8-Ball." Korey didn't say if any politicians were among the buyers.

Language: One name for the triangular-shaped parts of the die that provide answers is the *Spirit Slate*.

Marbles

The urge to flick small spherical objects at other little spheres must be common throughout humankind. How else could so many different societies have separately come up with marbles?

Egyptians, Aztecs, ancient Greeks, Syrians, and Romans are just a sample of ancient marble aficionados. The Romans in particular showed a particular panache for marbles—or as they called the game, *nuces*. The balls, so to speak, tended to be acorns or some other form of nut (*nuces* means "nuts" in Latin), but the contests were remarkably similar to some of today's marble contests. The game was so widespread that it's widely believed that Augustus Caesar was an avid nuces player in his youthful days before taking the throne. The great Roman writer Ovid is even credited with a poem explaining the rules of the game. (For those Ovid fans out there who believe setting the rules of marbles was beneath him, you have company, as some modern experts argue an unknown scribe actually penned the poem.)

The game eventually spread to France (where a marble was called a *bille*, or "little ball"), Holland (known as *knikkers*), and Britain, where *bowls* or *knickers* made enough of an impression on Shakespeare that he referenced a marbles game called *cherry pit* in the comedy *Twelfth Night*. But the European hub for marble making was undoubtedly Germany. The term *marbles* came into the common lexicon thanks to German exports of marble-fashioned balls to England at the beginning of the 1700s.

In America, the game didn't always receive a warm welcome. In 1882, a Virginian Baptist minister required a group of twenty-two converts to pledge "in the presence of God not to play ball or play marbles." Six years later, a group of Kansas City, Missouri, principals contemplated outlawing marbles. The concern was that playing for "keeps," wherein kids who won games earned the opponents' marbles, was "positively immoral and decidedly vicious and demoralizing in all its tendencies." Even cosmopolitan New York City couldn't avoid the scourge that was marbles. In 1894, the police were called to arrest a group of boys for playing marbles. The man who called the authorities explained his actions by telling the boys, "You haven't any business to play . . . You are on the road to perdition."

Marbles' image needed a good polishing and it came in the form of two savvy ball makers. The first was Samuel C. Dyke. The Akron, Ohio, native innovated mass production techniques and, equally important, was a great salesman. Originally a newspaperman, Dyke used the media to push his product. He helped set up tournaments—including a national event—and sold marble playing as a wholesome hobby at the start of the twentieth century.

Dyke died in 1924, but a worthy successor would soon enter the marble-making business. In the marbles world, Berry Pink was equal parts Pied Piper and P. T. Barnum. He dubbed himself "the Marble King" and named his company Marble King Inc. Pink marketed marbles with unending zeal. Like Dyke, he sponsored tournaments throughout the country, spending some $55,000 annually on prizes. He also went to schools and regularly gave away packs of marbles. He estimated that he gave away more than 50 million marbles during his lifetime. His greatest showpiece was a touring marbles exhibit. The *New York Post* gushed in 1938 that Berry had "marbles of jade and emerald, of silver and gold. He has one from King Tut's tomb, another from a crumbled Aztec palace." To whatever extent his questionable tales were true, he was an adroit businessman and helped spur an American marble-manufacturing boom.

But the dominance would not last. By the mid-1950s, cheaper Japanese marbles were putting American companies out of business. The Japanese had been introduced to marble making as part of the country's post–World War II reconstruction. Along with being less expensive, they were also quite beautiful. American marble manufacturers begged Congress to impose restrictive tariffs on foreign marbles in order to protect their business, but to no avail.

Today, Mexico and Asia account for the vast majority of marble manufacturing. As for Pink's Marble King Inc., it is one of the few American companies to survive. But to stay afloat, it's required the same business acumen that Pink showed some seventy years ago. Instead of only making marbles, his company has diversified into a slew of other areas including glass jewelry and glass tiles for home décor.

STATS AND FACTS

Dimensions: They tend to range from 0.5 inch in diameter to 1 inch, depending on whether they are a *shooter*, which the player flicks, or a target marble (known as a *mib*). Marbles with a diameter of less than 0.5 inch are called *peewees*, and some jumbo versions are 3 inches.

The Games: It's been estimated that there are at least 100 marble-based games. Versions include *pyramid* (aka *castle*), *nine holes*, *miniature marbles*, *bounce eye*, *ring taw*, and *egg in the bush*. *Ringer* is the most iconic: A 2- to 3-foot circle is drawn and players try to knock opponents' marbles out of the circle. The last shooter with marbles in the circle wins.

Idiomatic Phrases: Marbles have led to at least three famous phrases in popular culture: "playing for keeps" (typically winners get to keep the marbles of the losers); "knuckling down" (this relates to the technique of "shooting" a ball); and "losing your marbles" (also relates to the winner-take-all approach to play; the meaning shifted at the end of the nineteenth century from meaning losing one's temper to losing one's mind).

Strange But True: An English gardener named Jim "Atomic Thumb" Longhurst (born 1893) was such an adept marbles player that he was famous for his ability to shatter a pint glass with a marble shot from 4 feet away.

Language: Like the games, the balls also have unique names. Along with the famed *cat's eye* (clear with a colorful center), there are the *milkie* and the *purie*. These are made of one color; milkies are clear and generally white, while puries are opaque. *Crockies* are glazed stoneware such as china and porcelain. *Aggies*, which come from the word *agate*, describe marbles made from a natural mineral. Imitation aggies are known as *immies*.

PRESIDENTIAL BALLS

Maybe it's due to their competitive nature, but presidents love their ball games. Herbert Hoover relied heavily on his medicine ball (see page 98), while Rutherford B. Hayes endured scandal thanks to his affinity for quality croquet balls (see page 43). Here are five other oval office ballplayers:

1. Chester A. Arthur (marbles): While he probably didn't continue to play the game as an adult, Arthur was known to knock around the little spheres as a child. One 1883 *New York Times* article actually claimed the

continues . . .

. . . continued from previous page

future president had an unlikely chance encounter with James Garfield during a game of marbles when they were both kids. The two would run on the same ticket in 1880, and after Garfield was assassinated, Arthur would replace Garfield in the Oval Office.

2. George H.W. Bush (baseball): His son (and forty-third president) George Walker once co-owned a baseball team—the Texas Rangers—but the elder Bush was a solid college ballplayer. While serving as team captain at Yale, he played in both the 1947 and 1948 College World Series. He was known as a top-notch defensive first baseman.

3. Gerald R. Ford (golf): Though many presidents have taken to the links, Ford was probably the most lighthearted duffer. He had a penchant for mistakenly hitting balls into the gallery and once quipped: "I would like to deny all allegations by Bob Hope that during my last game of golf, I hit an eagle, a birdie, an elk, and a moose." Despite Ford's self-deprecation, *Golf Digest* once ranked him the third-best presidential golfer of all time (behind John F. Kennedy and Dwight Eisenhower).

4. Abraham Lincoln (billiards): Lincoln was described by others as a "respectable" pool player. Late in life, he referred to himself as a "billiards addict." The revered leader once lauded the sport, calling billiards "a health-inspiring scientific game, lending recreation to the otherwise fatigued mind."

5. Barack Obama (basketball): Obama has been a recreational basketball player his whole life—and apparently a pretty good one. He once engaged in a televised shooting contest with former college star and National Basketball Association player Clark Kellogg. After falling behind, the president said on CBS, "I'm not going to be humiliated on national television," and went on to win the game.

Mari

While the ball is usually the center of attention, the *mari* may be the only one that gets dolled up for its close-up with the public.

The Japanese pastime of *kemari* is said to have come to the Land of the Rising Sun in the seventh century from China. A game that teaches camaraderie, it's basically Hacky Sack with a soccer-sized ball. A group of six to eight players stand in a circle and attempt to keep the *mari* (Japanese for "ball") in the air with just the use of their right foot. (In modern times, a rally of twenty kicks could be considered a good performance.)

Made from deerskin and filled with beans, the ball is crafted with ever-loving care. According to one Western traveler in 1937, the balls have been manufactured following a traditional process perfected in the Kyoto region of

Japan, where kemari first came to the island nation. Most notably, the ball gets an exterior touch-up complete with white powder (described as "face powder" by our intrepid 1930s reporter), glue, and egg whites.

Despite the ball's star quality, kemari began to fall out of favor by the nineteenth century. The game did have one important patron: Emperor Meiji. Credited with bringing Japan into the modern industrial era, the emperor picked up a penchant for this ancient foot game while living in Hiroshima during the Sino-Japanese War (1894–1895). When kemari appeared to be almost gone by the start of the twentieth century, the Japanese leader stepped in. He insisted that a group of Kyoto aristocrats preserve the pastime. As a result, in 1903, a special society—funded by the emperor—was founded to preserve the tradition. (Today, the group still gets government funding through the Imperial Household Agency.)

The organization has dutifully maintained kemari— though for foreigners the game may look more like Kabuki than an actual sport. During demonstrations, the mari takes center stage riding a tree branch and is then offered to the shrine's altar with prayers for peace, prosperity, and a bountiful harvest.

Players are dressed in ornate costumes, which have varied in significance over time. When the samurai spread the game through the country in the thirteenth century, the colors could reflect skill level. Centuries later, the outfits distinguished the nobility from the commoners as the sport ultimately became a game for all social classes. As for the court, it's a 49-square-foot area marked off by four trees: a cherry for spring, willow for summer, maple for autumn, and pine for winter.

Yet even with all the high-value production, the mari doesn't keep itself up in the air. For that, players work hard on technique. "An ideal flick of the ball contains a moderate spin, makes a clear sound like a tsuzumi drum and should not be too low or too high," one player explained. Apparently, even stars get kicked around sometimes.

STATS AND FACTS

Dimensions: As the mari isn't mass-produced, the ball specs can vary. Still, it generally weighs between 3.5 and 4.5 ounces and is 8 to 9 inches in diameter—similar to the 8.5-inch soccer ball.

Historical Politics: The game is credited with bringing together two key noblemen who spurred important economic and land ownership changes known as the Taika Reforms in 645.

Modern Politics: In 1992, President George H.W. Bush tried his foot at kemari—the only problem is that he didn't stop there. A former high school soccer player, the elder Bush president began heading the ball, much to the chagrin of the traditional players.

Language: Modern players yell out the words *Ari*, *Yaa*, and *Ou* when kicking the ball. These are the names of the gods who came to the kemari Saint Fujiwara no Narimichi during a dream following 1,000 days of prayer.

Medicine ball

If you picture a bald strong man sporting a handlebar mustache and wearing a unitard when you hear the term *medicine ball*, you're probably not alone. In the beginning

of the twentieth century, the medicine ball gained favor in the United States as an all-purpose tool for overall fitness. The heavy ball, which could weigh up to 200 pounds, also became a staple training device for boxers from real-life heavyweight champion Jack Johnson in the first decades of the 1900s to the fictional Rocky Balboa of film fame more than a half-century later.

But the medicine ball's history spans thousands of years. The term *medicine ball* was first added to the English dictionary in 1895 as an entry for a "stuffed leather ball used for exercise." Nevertheless, the use of a spherical bladder full of sand to add weight was employed as far back as 1000 BC by Persian soldiers as part of training regimes. During the Greek era, the famed physician Hippocrates incorporated the ball's use in his prescriptions for conditioning and rehabilitation, and Renaissance physician Hieronymus Mercurialis endorsed them as part of a "medicinal gymnastics" program—hence, the origins of the term *medicine ball*.

Outside the training arena, it became an object for innovation at, of all places, the White House. While U.S. President Herbert Hoover struggled to solve the economic depression, he embraced the weighted orb as part of a new sport dubbed *Hoover-ball* by the *New York Times*. Created in 1931 by White House doctor Admiral Joel T. Boone to keep the beefy president fit, the game was a hybrid of tennis and volleyball—only with a medicine ball. Teams of two to four players would throw a 6-pound heavy ball over an 8-foot-high net on a tennis-like court. One of the opponents would have to catch the ball and immediately try to throw it over to an unplayable spot. If the ball hit the ground, a point was won; the game was scored like tennis.

"It required less skill than tennis, was faster and more vigorous, and therefore gave more exercise in a short time," wrote Hoover in his memoirs. Not surprisingly, the history of Hoover-ball is about as memorable as Hoover's difficult tenure in the Oval Office.

The ball has also been used in a military game called *bull in the ring*, which is essentially a he-man version of keep away, featuring soldiers tossing the medicine ball around past a fellow grunt in the center of a circle.

Today, medicine balls are still a popular core strength training tool and can be found at a range of weights generally varying from 2 to 35 pounds. A number of different manufacturing styles are used, with grippable polyurethane, vinyl, or leather outer shells being the most popular and sand, silicone, or rubber chips creating the weight inside.

STATS AND FACTS

Dimensions: There are various sizes, but the traditional medicine ball is similar in shape to a basketball—between 27 and 29 inches in circumference.

American Debut: The first known sighting of a medicine ball in the United States is a photo of Harvard College Gymnasium curator Aaron Molyneaux Hewlett at his desk at some point between 1859 and 1871.

Language: It's known as the *med ball* for short; in the early twentieth century, the medicine ball was dubbed one of the *Four Horsemen of Fitness* along with the dumbbell and two forgotten fitness instruments: the Indian club and the wand.

Meditation balls

Dating back to China's Ming Dynasty (AD 1368–1644), these balls have gone by many names—*mediation balls, Baoding balls, Chinese healthy balls, relaxation harmony balls, Chinese iron balls, meridian balls,* and *Qigong balls,* to name a few. Whatever the title, the purpose of the handheld orbs—generally sold in pairs and used by rotating them in one's hand—is the same. They serve as a healing, calming, or exercise device.

The balls' origin can be traced to the city of Baoding in China's Hebei province. Artisans in the area began making the orbs out of solid iron as a way to either

strengthen hands following injury or as a tool for improving manual dexterity. At some point during the Qing Dynasty (1644–1912), the design had changed. The balls were still commonly created out of iron and later steel (though semiprecious stones such as jade or finely finished wood were also used), but they were hollow with a sounding plate inside. The chimes offer both a low and a high tone, which are said to represent yin and yang.

These balls were not just for the old or frail. Versions were used centuries ago by warriors as weapons and by acrobats to show their skill and flexibility. But in Chinese medicine they provide a more nurturing purpose. It is believed that our hands serve as a healing gateway to both the brain and vital organs. Using these balls, this line of thinking goes, can help with everything from hypertension to liver disorders.

Lest you assume meditation balls do not have a role in modern sports, think again. In a 1996 issue of *Black Belt* magazine, the balls were heartily recommended as a training device. The article boasted that the balls can help a martial artist adopt the characteristics of a tiger. "The fingers can be strengthened so they can serve effectively as claws . . . by [among other methods] constantly conditioning them with the Chinese iron balls training device," the journalist wrote.

Even athletes who aren't aiming for tiger claws have enjoyed these balls' benefit. In 1986, Philadelphia Eagles quarterback Randall Cunningham severely bruised his thumb and was questionable for the team's final two games of the season. Cunningham was given a pair of Chinese healthy balls, which he credited for enabling him to play in the team's final contest. It's unclear just how much the balls helped as the Eagles fell to the Washington Redskins 21–14.

Former Dallas Cowboys' backup quarterback (and the team's future head coach) Jason Garrett was also a proponent. Following the 1994 season, in which the Cowboys won a division title and made it to the conference finals, Garrett presented each member of the squad's offensive line with silver meditation balls. Garrett, who saw action in just two of the team's sixteen regular-season games, admitted that the balls were not the most ostentatious gift. When informed by the media that starting quarterback Troy Aikman gave each lineman a round-trip ticket to anywhere in the United States and cowboy boots, Garrett deadpanned: "Troy can afford the plane tickets better than I can."

STATS AND FACTS

Dimensions: The size and the weight of the balls differ. Therapeutically, larger, heavier balls offer the most stimulation, but experts recommend that beginners start with smaller versions. Balls tend to range from 1.5 to 2.1875 inches in diameter and weights also vary depending on the materials used. For example, a set of solid jade balls, which are a little more than 2 inches in diameter, weighs approximately 1 pound.

Presidential Connection: During a 1984 trip to China, President Ronald Reagan received a set of meditation balls from Chinese Premier Zhao Ziyang. The reason for the gift: The balls were "given to older men to roll around in their palms so they can head off arthritis," the *Los Angeles Times* explained.

Language: *Jingluo* is the Chinese medical system outlining how the ten fingers in the hand serve as a network of bodily energy. The medicinal use of meditation balls is based on this theory.

Nerf ball

Although *Nerf* may seem more like a franchise nowadays, it started as a single squishy softball-sized ball. In fact, it really started in 1968 as a foam rock. *Nerf ball* inventor Reyn Guyer originally planned to use the spongy polyurethane as part of a new game called *Caveman*. In it, players would throw faux boulders at opponents to prevent them from stealing pretend money. The premise might sound odd—cavemen with money and all—but Guyer had come up with the bestselling game *Twister* two years earlier so some respect must be given to his creative process.

Thankfully for the sporting world, during *Caveman* testing, he realized that it was more fun throwing the soft injury-proof rocks around than it was playing his game. A little cutting here and there, and eureka—the Nerf ball was born. Well, actually the *Muffball*—as it was original called—was born. Despite his enthusiasm for the new orb, the ball was initially only part of his master plan. Experienced in the game industry, Guyer was convinced that he couldn't get a company to buy just a light foam ball. Instead, he packaged it as part of an indoor set that allowed users to play outdoor games such as volleyball and basketball inside the house. Milton Bradley, which had cashed in on Guyer's *Twister*, passed. But the company's biggest competitor, Parker Brothers, embraced it.

After swooping in, Parker Brothers execs starting realizing what Guyer had seen: The ball itself—without any games attached—was a marketable product. After one session in which some testers enjoyed a rousing game of throwing the sphere at each other, they came to the conclusion that the biggest selling point was a ball that wouldn't wreck a home. The old maternal missive "don't play ball in the house" could be ditched.

But finding a name for the ball wasn't a slam dunk. The Muffball was chucked. Parker Brothers considered such titles as *Orbie* and the *Moonball*. It was 1969, the year of the first lunar landing, so an outer-space theme made sense. Ultimately, the title came from Earth. The word *nerf* had been used in the car racing industry since the 1940s. In the 1960s, a *nerf bar* was the name for metal tubing attached to the chassis of hot rods. The device helped protect the vehicle. The sound of nerf resonated with the Parker Brothers executives. "Nerf rolled off the tongue all round and cushiony, like the product itself," wrote Ellen Wojahn in her book *The General Mills/Parker Brothers Merger: Playing by Different Rules.*

As is often the case with innovation, many retailers were skeptical about the Nerf ball. One department store chain refused to carry the sphere, claiming it was overpriced at around $1 and its simplicity offended the intelligence of buyers. Minds were quickly changed when the ball became a nationwide hit in 1970. In that first year on the market, more than 4 million Nerf balls were sold.

The ball was great indoors, but the lightweight sphere wasn't something you wanted to use outside. It just didn't have enough heft to handle midrange throws or windy weather. Parker Brothers quickly noted the problem. They consulted a foam armrest manufacturer from the car industry about ways to make a more durable, somewhat heavier ball. The answer came in the form of liquid molded foam. Using the new technology, the Nerf football was unveiled in 1972. Perfect for kids who wanted a smaller version of the traditional pigskin (it was three-quarters the size of the standard ball), the Nerf creation became a staple for playground football games.

Nerf was now established both inside and out. From there, Parker Brothers kept adding to the line. Nerf material has been used to make such oddball items as a kid's vehicle, a superhero costume, and a glider. Sports balls that have been translated into Nerf products include table tennis balls, billiard balls, soccer balls, golf balls, and basketballs. Toy guns using Nerf ammunition have been a big hit. "Nerf started as a nonsense word and turned into an umbrella word," one Parker Brothers executive rightly concluded.

STATS AND FACTS

Dimensions: The original ball is 3.75 inches in diameter and weighs approximately 12 grams.

Colors: The first ball came in one of four colors: blue, red, orange, or yellow. The initial Nerf football was offered in such flamboyant hues as "Orange Squeezer," "Limebacker," and "Purple Passer."

Language: Inspired by the ball, *to nerf* in the fantasy gaming world (such as the online role-playing game *World of Warcraft*) means to weaken the abilities of a character or object in the game. For example, asking game architects "to nerf" a wizard would be a request to cut down on that character's powers.

Netball

The sport of netball was invented almost by accident. Its ball was likely a product of unexpected circumstance as well. A Louisiana teacher named Clara Baer inadvertently started a new sport when she misinterpreted the rules of basketball sent to her by the game's inventor, James Naismith. Baer's version, dubbed *Basquette*, was designed in 1895 for women athletes. It utilized hoops (no backboards) and probably employed basketballs, which were invented a couple years earlier (though lighter soccer balls might have been used). The main differences: Players were confined to certain zones on the court and the sport didn't allow for dribbling or guarding opponents.

It turns out that the game traveled well. Baer's creation spread to England, where it was embraced and sent throughout the empire modified and rebranded as netball. (It remains particularly popular in England, Australia, and New Zealand with more than 20 million playing the sport worldwide.) Basketballs weren't plentiful abroad at the start of the twentieth century so even if they had been initially used for Baer's game, they were probably passed over for the ubiquitous soccer ball in the game's transatlantic voyage.

Though different than its soccer cousin, the current netball appears to have drawn more inspiration from the soccer ball than the basketball. The netball's typical eighteen-panel configuration looks a little like an old-time soccer ball. It's also the same size as a modern full-sized soccer ball. Nevertheless, the orb has its own personality. The outer casing typically includes a unique grip-friendly surface and, increasingly, features designs with pizzazz—from hot pink to funky green and yellow patterns. Still, style never gets in the way of substance. Simple white balls are available and manufacturers who add a little zest are careful to choose looks with some level of symmetry. This ensures that the ball will appear rounder when rotating through the air—a factor more important than pretty balls.

STATS AND FACTS

Dimensions: Official netballs are 27 to 28 inches in circumference and weigh 14 to 16 ounces.

Language: Each netball player must wear a *bib*, which looks like a colored sleeveless undershirt rather than what's worn by a baby. The pullover indicates a player's position and where she's allowed to go on the court.

Paintballs

Assuming you don't count water balloons, the paintball is sport's lone ball that is only a success when it breaks. Figuring out how to perfect that task has been a huge part of the evolution of this pint-sized projectile.

Paintballers need to give the U.S. Forest Service a tip of the gun for indirectly starting the paintball craze. In the early 1960s, the government asked a chemist named

Charles Nelson and his brother to come up with a paint-filled pellet that could be used to mark trees from a distance. The little wax numbers they invented did the trick. Shot from guns known as *markers*, they proved so useful that they were also used by ranchers, who would shoot their cattle for identification purposes.

But these early projectiles would have never been used for hunting friends in a playful paintball game. Though the cows never complained, by all accounts the hard-hitting wax pellets were not something you'd want to be struck with. That changed thanks to R. P. Scherer, a big pharmaceutical company that had made a mint by inventing soft-gel capsules for pills and suppositories. They figured gelatin balls might be a little more efficient than wax pellets and began selling their prototype as a casing for paint-filled ammunition. At the time, R. P. Scherer probably didn't see the paintball invention as a big moneymaker. In fact, the first company to design a paintball gun stopped production when it found the process a financially unsound venture.

Enter just the right group of men to create the game of paintball—smart guys who liked to argue. In 1981, these fellas wanted to settle a debate as to whether country folk or urban dwellers had better survival skills. To answer the question, they traveled to a 125-acre wood in New Hampshire decked out in goggles, camouflage outfits, and most important, packing Nel-Spot 007 bolt-action paintball pistols (made by Nelson's company) with approximately twenty balls of paint apiece. One participant, *Pumping Iron* author Charlie Gaines, would later describe the guns as "temperamental." As for the white paint–filled balls, they were also unreliable as some didn't burst on contact. In the end, a keen New England outdoorsman named Ritchie White beat those from the concrete jungle without ever firing a shot.

Originally dubbed the "National Survival Game" by the guys, the concept would soon morph into paintball. Early gamers could not have been happy with the original paintballs. The oil-based paints used in the balls couldn't be washed out. Solving this quandary was no easy task. Because the paintball's gelatinous casing was water soluble, a water-based paint—the kind that easily washes off—could prove problematic, swelling up or even melting away the outer casing. The perfect paintball would have to be nonstaining yet thick enough to provide a visible mark on the target. The eureka moment came in 1985 in the form of a "nonionic polyoxyethylene derivative of fatty acid partial esters of sorbitol anhydride." Practically speaking, the new sphere meant that players could easily scrub away the paintball residue after a day on the range.

Modern paintballs aren't for the weak hearted. They are fired at a velocity of 126 miles per hour, giving them a range of approximately 100 yards. *Popular Mechanics* estimated that at 30 yards a crack shot should be pretty accurate with a paintball gun, but that at 50 yards even the most skilled player will have difficulty hitting an opponent. Nevertheless, the speed at which a paintball can be fired is limited in most places as a ball fired at current maximum velocities will usually leave a red welt. Good players can fire off twenty or more balls per second with chip-controlled markers, and if getting splattered is not enough, balls are now on the market in a variety of scents. So if the yellow paint doesn't tell you who the loser is, the smell of bananas will.

STATS AND FACTS

Dimensions: 0.68 inch in diameter (.68 caliber) and 3.2 grams.

Strange But True: Paintballs' gelatin capsules are made from animal products. For some vegans, this has served as an obstacle to getting into the sport. As a result, in 2009, one team of enterprising Purdue University students designed a machine that can produce animal-free paintballs.

Language: *Bonus balls* are paintballs that hit competitors after they are officially out of the contest. (This can happen by accident because of the speed paintballs fly out of the gun or because a player leaves the battlefield too slowly. It can also be done to annoy the disqualified opponent.) This is also known as *extra love*.

Pallo

In the 1900s, a Finnish athlete and future professor named Lauri "Tahko" Pihkala witnessed the game of baseball and liked what he saw—to a degree. He thought the game was a little too slow and figured if he made a few tweaks his fellow countrymen would embrace the sport. The result was *pesäpallo*, a sport that to most Americans would appear like bizarro baseball. There are nine players on a side, innings, outs, a batter, a pitcher, gloves, and bats. But the bases are in a zigzag configuration of varying lengths; the pitch is lobbed to the hitter; the bat is long and skinny and often made of fiberglass; and even smacking the ball out of the park is a no-no (it's just a foul).

As for the ball itself, forget baseball's white sphere with red stitching. The *pallo* (Finnish for "ball") is a totally different beast than its American cousin. Despite the game's baseball roots, organizers actually drew inspiration from the bandy ball (see page 7). The result, according to a *New York Daily Mirror* reporter in 1939, was a ball "more like an Irish hurley ball, being lighter and less lively than a baseball." Though the Finns went their own way with the ball, it was far from perfect. Early versions were known to unravel, requiring design upgrades.

Perfecting the sphere, which is now smaller and heavier than a baseball and features seams like a tennis ball, has been a priority for the game. In 2003, the pesäpallo federation went so far as to employ Finland's research institute for Olympic sports to get the ball bouncing right. Traditionally, the pallo had rules for weight and circumference, but nothing on its elasticity. As a result, some companies would produce a high-flying orb, while others would manufacture a dead fish. The Finnish institute pulled out a large pneumatic gun and started firing balls at a wall to figure out just the right bounce for the pallo. After they produced a fifteen-page report on the topic, the game's governing body started requiring ball producers

RECORD BALLS

For some unknown reason, people who want to set records often gravitate to balls. The following is a sampling of some ball-related feats. As people have a fixation on ball records, these marks may have already been broken by the time you read this.

1. *Basketball*: A Florida man spun twenty-eight basketballs simultaneously in a 1999 London exhibition. Sitting down, he mainly used a contraption on his leg to balance the spinning spheres, but he also had balls going on his head and fingers.

2. *Golf ball*: The record for most golf balls hit in a 12-hour span was set in 2010 in Florida. The total: 7,721.

3. *Soccer ball*: In 2004, a Swedish man kept a soccer ball in the air for 8 hours, 32 minutes, and 3 seconds without letting it drop once.

4. *Space Hopper*: A New Yorker set the record in 2010 for the fastest mile on a Space Hopper. His time: 13 minutes flat.

5. *Tennis ball*: The longest singles tennis marathon occurred in 2010 in Germany. Two men hit a ball back and forth for 55 hours, 55 minutes, and 55 seconds straight. The record doesn't indicate how many different balls were used during the rally.

to make versions with uniform hop. Nevertheless, the fine-tuned pallo remains a long way off from a baseball.

STATS AND FACTS

Dimensions: The pallo must be between approximately 8.5 and 8.85 inches in circumference. Weights vary depending on who is playing. A men's ball is about 5.5 to 5.8 ounces. Women's and kids' pallos are progressively lighter.

American Perspective: When the Finnish included pesäpallo as an exhibition sport at the 1952 Helsinki Olympic Games, famed sports writer Red Smith was not impressed. The writer quipped that the sport "was invented by Lauri [Pihkala], a professor who wears a hearing aid.... Somebody must have described baseball to him when his battery was dead."

World Interest: Although it's a Finnish game, pesäpallo has spread to other parts of the globe, including Australia, Canada, Sweden, and Germany.

Language: A *kunnari* is a home run. But keeping with the game's slightly askew view of baseball, a batter only needs to reach third base in order to accomplish the feat.

Pétanque boules

The Capulets and the Montagues, the Hatfields and the McCoys ... the Blancs and the Souvignets? In France, where the sport of *pétanque* has deep roots, one familial feud has stood out above the others.

Invented in 1907, pétanque is France's most popular version of the age-old game bocce (see page 34). In contrast to bocce, French players are required to throw the

ball at a target with their *pieds tanqués*—translated into English as "legs together." This was shortened to pétanque and used as the game's name. Ball construction is another key difference. In the early days, nails were hammered into a wooden ball to create a metal sphere (bocce is played with wooden balls). Needless to say, these studded boules weren't too efficient, and as a result, Jean Blanc—the head of the Blanc family—entered the pétanque scene.

Blanc and a partner began producing hollow steel balls in Blanc's tiny southern Loire Valley village of Saint-Bonnet-le-Château in 1927. These proved a hit and for nearly three decades his brand called JB established itself as the leader in boules manufacturing. Surely, Blanc expected that he would eventually have serious competition in the metal boules market, but it must have come as a surprise when a local locksmith named Frederic Bayet entered the boules-making business in 1955. Though Saint-Bonnet-le-Château only has around 1,600 residents, it now had two companies competing for boules supremacy: JB and Bayet's Obut.

Blanc may have had a head start, but Bayet had Jean Souvignet and his sons, Georges and Robert. The Souvignets had extensive metalworking experience, and under their stewardship, Obut surpassed JB. The tension between the family-run companies—which had become the top two boules producers in the world—continued to boil through the years. "At one point in the '80s, when Far Eastern competition was at its strongest," Obut's Pierre Souvignet once explained, "we entered a price war which was destructive to both companies."

Despite the conflict, unlike Shakespeare's fictional Italian families in *Romeo and Juliet* or nineteenth-century gun-toting Appalachian backcountry folk, the Blancs and the Souvignets had a more strategic way of dealing with their differences. In 1995, the son of the managing director of Obut married the daughter of JB's head. While both companies still produce their own line of balls, the nuptials led to a détente.

The companies could now concentrate on a combined enemy: Asia. Three years after the Blanc-Souvignet wedding, the French boules industry (of which Obut and JB had an 80 percent market share) convinced the French government to put stringent regulations on importing Asian boules. The companies successfully argued that many foreign boules were made of thin alloys and were then stuffed with such ingredients as sand, clay, or mercury to bring them up to throwing weight. (Proper boules should be hollow in the center with a thick metal outer shell.) When these substandard balls collided, they sometimes exploded, sending shrapnel everywhere. The protection certainly didn't hurt as Obut and JB continue to lead the way in the boules industry. Today, Obut boasts a production of 300,000 boules per month.

But even with governmental assistance, the Saint-Bonnet-le-Château companies didn't slack. Their ball-making specs are exacting. Obut, for example, offers 1,200 different sets of boules. Each set has slightly different weight and size combinations. Boules are made from at least a dozen different grades of steel, and companies carefully guard their formulas as each unique composition offers a different feel in the hand. The choice of steel (and other properties) just depends on the boules player— as does whether to support team Blanc or team Souvignet.

STATS AND FACTS

Dimensions: Each steel boules must be 2.77 to 3.15 inches in diameter and weigh between 1.43 and 1.76 pounds. The weight must come from the steel and not additives such as sand. The target ball, known as the *cochonnet* ("piglet" in French), ranges from 0.98 to 1.38 inches in diameter.

Language: The game has a tradition known as *kissing fanny*. Legend has it that this custom started in the South of France following World War I. Feeling sorry for players who lost 13–0 in a game of pétanque, a local waitress allowed the loser to give her a kiss on the cheek. When the mayor was defeated by a lopsided score, the saucy waitress offered up another cheek to kiss. The mayor obliged, and to this day, many pétanque playing areas have the likeness of a woman's derrière nearby for any player to smooch following an embarrassing shutout.

Pinball

Could Marie Antoinette have been a pinball wizard? It's possible; although instead of the silver ball, she would have been playing with ivory. Pinball's forerunner—

bagatelle—was a game of kings in the eighteenth century. Louis XVI's brother, the Count D'Atrois, was a big player, and any party at his aptly named Chateau de Bagatelle in Paris—which the king and queen were known to have attended before their eventual date with the guillotine— included some time enjoying the game.

Played on a narrow, angled billiard table, competitors used billiards cues and took turns shooting ivory balls at holes with different scores attached depending on the difficulty of the shot. It was a nice change of pace from billiards and spread to both Great Britain and the United States. The game developed enough popularity that a famous 1864 Currier and Ives political cartoon of Abraham Lincoln had the future president lining up an ivory ball.

Considering the cost of equipment, the game was most likely a pursuit of the well heeled. To bring the game to the masses, entrepreneurs rolled out smaller versions of the pastime in America in the late nineteenth century—a period where innovation also led to spring-loaded plungers replacing pool sticks. By the beginning of the twentieth century, variations of this scaled-down game were popular, with marbles of differing consistencies replacing the larger ivory balls on the smaller table.

The modern pinball game was ultimately a product of economic circumstance. During the Great Depression, small struggling stores found that pinball-like machines were good moneymakers. These contraptions went by a variety of names in the early days, with two of the most popular being Baffle Ball and Ballyhoo. With pins being added to the table to move the ball in unpredictable ways, a Louisville, Kentucky, newspaper dubbed these "pin-and-ball" games. Ultimately, a Louisville judge apparently shortened it to "pinball."

The famed silver ball, which is basically a large bearing ball, developed into a regular part of the game in 1934. It's unclear why it became the industry-wide standard. Marc Schoenberg, an executive at Stern Pinball Inc., suggests designers figured these supersized metal marbles just moved best around the playing field. Having one ball of universal design also made it easy for all brands to quickly replace balls that became unplayable. After that momentous decision, most of the game's changes came in the form of what moved the ball around the playing area. Bouncy bumpers were added in 1937 and flippers came along a decade later.

These additions were essential because originally a player would simply insert money, send the ball on its way, and hope for the best. Government officials saw this level of chance as simply gambling because most pinball machines offered either cash jackpots or free games for high scores. As a result, cities like New York and Los Angeles took the serious step of banning pinball in the late 1930s and early 1940s. New York City Mayor Fiorello La Guardia once went as far as to take a sledgehammer to confiscated pinball machines. Even the Kennedys had issues. As U.S. Attorney General, Robert F. Kennedy claimed that the game was not only akin to slot machines, but the pinball industry was also the domain of organized crime.

Then came the Who's 1969 hit single "Pinball Wizard," which raised the game's cool quotient above the complaints of politicians. Amazingly, it was pure luck that the silver ball ever got an anthem. Quite simply, an influential rock critic loved pinball and suggested a good review might be in the offing if the band added a song about the game to its rock opera, *Tommy*. "I wrote 'Pinball Wizard' purely as a scam," the Who's Peter Townshend would tell *Uncut* magazine in 2004.

For the next decade, the game enjoyed a golden age. But the advent of *Pong*, *Space Invaders*, and *Pac-Man* crushed pinball. In 1979, Bally, which was an industry leader, reported revenues of $129 million. Two years later, as video games started dominating arcades, they pulled in half that amount.

During these tumultuous times, the ball itself has seen little change. The standard is made of carbon steel. Chrome steel, which is more finely polished and lasts longer than carbon variants, is also used. But they are not as common because their polarity makes them unusable in machines featuring magnets. A third option is a ceramic ball. These spheres—called *powerballs*—are the same size as their steel cousins but are considerably lighter. Alas, the hope nowadays for those who love these machines is that these balls don't become just a relic from a fading rock song.

STATS AND FACTS

Dimensions: The standard pinball is 1.0625 inches in diameter and weighs 2.8 ounces. The ceramic power ball is the same diameter but weighs 2.29 ounces.

Language: The term *tilt* is used when a player moves a machine to alter the direction of the ball. A player who tilts a machine forfeits the game. The word was first used for this purpose by prominent pinball maker Harry Williams. "I saw people trying to lift the machines to get the ball into the high scoring holes," Williams said. "I called the first tilt mechanism 'stool pigeon.' Then one day someone was playing and he said, 'Damn it, I tilted it' and I thought to myself, 'That's perfect.'"

Pink ball (Spaldeen, Pennsy Pinky)

Nearly every morning he was home during the 1951 Major League Baseball season, Willie Mays had a date with a pink ball. One of baseball's greatest players would be woken by kids in his New York neighborhood of Harlem and cajoled into playing a game of the urban street world's version of baseball—*stickball*. At the center of

each of those games was a hollow, rubber pink ball. Most likely, it was a *Spaldeen*, New York parlance for the *Spalding High-Bounce Ball*, or possibly it was a *Pennsy Pinky*, an alternative brand manufactured by the Penn tennis equipment company. After a rousing game, the future Hall of Famer would buy popsicles or ice cream for the kids and then head to the Polo Grounds to shine in his day job as the center fielder for the New York Giants.

While Mays is perhaps the greatest practitioner of the Spaldeen, countless children throughout America's large cities relied on the ball for their summer entertainment in the fifties, sixties, and seventies. Other future big league baseball players, like Phil Rizzuto, Joe Torre, and Willie Randolph, began their careers playing stickball. But regular kids were equally smitten with the pink ball. "[T]he Spaldeen was at the heart of most of the games, and near the end of the day we would prowl the rooftops looking for balls that had been caught in drains, wedged behind pigeon coops, stuck under slats or behind chimneys," Pete Hamill, a prominent journalist and author, reminisced in a 1980 *New York* magazine article.

The original Spaldeen was created by many, many mistakes. During the tennis ball production process, Spalding would have to discard spheres with slight defects. For those orbs blemished before receiving their fuzzy outer coat, the company decided to rebrand them "Spalding High-Bounce" and position them as inexpensive kids' balls. In 1949, they went on the market at corner drugstores and toy shops. Penn's version followed later. Spalding, Penn, and other ball makers would soon see the value of their creation, ditching the defective balls and manufacturing better-quality versions.

Pink balls were perfect for kids living in the country's ever-growing concrete jungles following World War II. They had great bounce but were soft enough that they wouldn't do the kind of damage a baseball or even a tennis ball might cause. The versatility of the ball led to as many games as the imagination could produce. Stickball had batters (usually using a skinny mop handle or broomstick) swinging away against a team of four or more players. (*Punchball* was a variation where the hand replaced the stick.) Most of the rules of baseball applied with one exception: If the ball traveled over a roof, it was an out—not a home run. The reason: "Because you'd lose the ball," explained Mays. "You [had] to hit for location."

Other popular games that emerged included *I declare war* in which players assumed the name of a country. In a show of hard diplomacy, the person with the ball would shout out, "I declare war on . . ." and then mention one of the chosen nations before pelting the opposition. *Stoopball* had competitors throwing the ball off the stairs leading to walk-up apartments. Players would attempt to snag the ball directly off the carom. A similar contest was *roofball*, in which the Spaldeen was chucked onto an angled roof and the goal was to catch the ball before it hit the ground.

For nearly three decades, the balls were ubiquitous, but the Spaldeen was discontinued in 1979 (most pundits blame video games). The Pennsy Pinky also left the market around the same time. Some brokenhearted Spaldeen aficionados were unwilling to go quietly. Robert DiFiore of Armonk, New York, began a cottage industry, producing homemade pink balls. His process included lining a clothes dryer with sandpaper and tossing a few dozen tennis balls in the machine on the fluff cycle for two days. "It made a mess with all the lint left in the dryer," he told the *New York Times* in 1999, "but it worked." Elsewhere, a company called Sky Bounce Inc. was manufacturing 200,000 balls a year in the mid-1990s and remains in business today.

Looking to tap into the pocketbooks of nostalgic baby boomers, Spalding brought the Spaldeen back in 1999. The new version was a replica of the original Spaldeen— the company even delved into its files in order to re-create the exact rubber formula that gave the original balls their pink hue and distinctive smell. (The *New York Times* called the odor "similar to that of new tires, but less aromatic.") Keeping with progress, the new Spaldeens were touted as far more durable than their predecessors. The company estimated that the new pink ball could handle 500 bounces against cement at 50 miles per hour before it became unusable.

In spite of the efforts, the ball didn't spark a full-scale return to street games. As a result, Spalding further emphasized the nostalgic value of the Spaldeen, selling it where the players of old probably shop today—stores like Bed, Bath & Beyond and Restoration Hardware.

STATS AND FACTS

Dimensions: Pink balls are typically about 2.5 inches in diameter and 3.2 ounces in weight.

Language: A *two-sewer man* was a stickball player who could smack a Spaldeen from one sewer manhole cover (which generally served as home plate) past two other covers. Many considered this a respectable feat as covers were located roughly 75 feet apart on the street. It was said that the greats like Willie Mays were *four-sewer men*, which meant they could send the soft pink ball some 300 feet.

Polo ball

It you want to understand where civilization started in ball development, check out polo. Thousands of years ago, men in Central Asia were competing in a folk fore-runner to modern polo called *buzkashi*. Players rode on horseback attempting to gallop victorious against an opposing team carrying the game's ball. The typical ball: a headless goat carcass (though a deceased duck or calf sans head were also sometimes used).

Progress came to the game—and its ball—thanks to

royal interest. An ancient plaque next to a polo ground north of Kashmir contains the following inscription: "Let other people play at other things. The king of games is still the game of kings." Indeed, Alexander the Great was supposedly an avid player. Upon ascending to the throne of Macedonia in 336 BC, he is said to have received a polo ball and mallet from Persian Emperor Darius III (the implication was that the new monarch should stick to games). Alexander mocked the gift, saying he represented the stick and the ball was the world he expected to conquer.

Persia (modern-day Iran), where the game was known as *chogan* or *chaughan*, was likely the cradle of the modern sport, but polo spread and other countries made contributions to its development. The Tibetans, who were early players, must have moved away from animal corpses, because their word *pulu* (or *po-lo*) means "willow root" and referred to the plant-based ball they used to play the game. Of course, the term eventually became the worldwide name of the game. Still, some regal players may have held on to the tradition of the sport's older balls. Legend claims the Mongols under the leadership of Genghis Kahn and Tamerlane used the decapitated heads of their enemies in heated polo matches.

The sport didn't reach the West until the late nineteenth century. British cavalrymen first laid eyes on the game while posted in Crimea in the 1850s. When they returned to England, the soldiers spent their idle time trying out the sport. They apparently used the ever-so-British cricket ball for their inaugural games. When the men shipped out to India, they continued to play the game with their colonial brethren.

The British Empire's great scribe Rudyard Kipling

wrote about polo—and expressed strong opinions about the ball's makeup. In his short story "The Maltese Cat" (1895), Kipling—as told through the perspective of a horse named the Maltese Cat—proclaimed "that bamboos grew solely in order that polo balls might be turned from their roots." It appears that India's polo association agreed because that organization required game balls be made of bamboo. Elsewhere, the English opted for willow (their rules mandated that the ball be slightly larger than a baseball), while America's governing body initially insisted on basswood.

While the differing consistencies did offer a range of resilience, every wood ball eventually had to be discarded because of either splits or dents from the constant pounding from polo mallets. An alternative emerged from the unlikely polo hotbed of Dallas, Texas. In the late 1970s Vincent Meyer took concepts he had developed while making a rustproof fertilizer spreader to produce one of the first plastic spheres that had the pop and feel of a wooden polo ball. These durable and perfectly round options did have one big downside. Whereas wood balls would whistle when struck, giving players an audible cue to get out of the way of a speeding ball, the plastic versions flew silently through the air. Nevertheless, the durability won out and wooden balls became a minority choice on polo fields.

The biggest losers in the move to plastics were those who had crafted polo balls for generations. An area of India near the city of Kolkata was once a center for handmade bamboo balls. By 2007, it only had one maker left. Historically, those local companies would engage in a labor-intensive process that required cutting the bamboo and letting the stumps sit for a year before they became cylindrical. Balls would then be chiseled out and made smooth with sandpaper. Now, the balls for the sport of kings are in the hands of, among others, a Texas fertilizer expert.

STATS AND FACTS

Dimensions: A polo ball is between 3 and 3.5 inches in diameter and weighs 4.5 to 4.75 ounces.

Variation: An indoor style of the game known as *arena polo* is played with an inflatable leather ball. At 14.5 inches in circumference, it's essentially the size of a large softball.

Language: A *chukker* is the term for a period in a polo match. A game usually has six *chukkers*, each lasting a specified amount of time (usually 7 minutes). The term comes from the Hindi word for "wheel."

Pushball (bladderball, cage ball)

As the second industrial revolution steamed along in the late nineteenth century, there was an urge in all facets of life to make things bigger and better (ships, bridges, buildings, you name it). Even the ball received supersized treatment.

In the early 1890s, Moses G. Crane, inventor of the fire alarm, had three sons playing football at Harvard University. While watching them in action, he wondered why the sport couldn't be played with a larger ball so that spectators could better follow the action. He posed his idea to the Newton (Massachusetts) Athletic Association in 1894 and within a year he'd come up with a new creation: the pushball.

In fact, it was literally a huge invention. The first ball, featuring a leather exterior covering a blown-up rubber bladder was 6 feet in diameter and weighed 70 pounds. Crane's invention caught the eye of just the right supporters—among them was sporting goods magnate Albert G. Spalding. Known for making equipment for nearly every American ball sport, Spalding applied his sales savvy to the pushball. He published a history/rule book on the behemoth ball and marketed an "official" Spalding pushball similar to Crane's original. In the code published by Spalding, the game was played in a manner similar to football with eleven players on a side trying to get the ball into a goal.

At around the same time, pushball was successfully introduced in both New York City and throughout England. Exhibitions were such a success in the Big Apple that pushball on horseback was introduced with much fanfare. Across the Atlantic, the British also took to the big ball. For example, the future King George VI reportedly played the game in his younger days.

Still, the game never truly captured the imagination of either country. It did secure a lasting legacy in two locations: military bases and college campuses. During both World Wars, Marine bases from American Lake, Washington, to Parris Island, South Carolina, used the ball. The game got even a bigger bounce from college coeds. For decades, the pushball was a staple for competitions between freshmen and sophomores at universities throughout the United States. The rules laid down at the start of the century weren't important. Instead, it was all about the pushball. As a result, these matches tended to be free-for-alls with throngs of battered and bruised participants representing each side.

Yale University put its own spin on the proceedings. In 1954, teams representing the school's media—the newspaper, the yearbook, the radio station, and the humor magazine—squared off using the big ball. Possibly because pushball started on the campus of its rival Harvard, the Yale organizers dubbed their game *bladderball*. The story of Yale's bladderball is instructive on the ultimate demise of pushball in the United States. As the country became more litigious, the big ball just seemed too dangerous. Ironically, a big ball fan—future Major League Baseball commissioner and then-Yale president A. Bartlett Giamatti—banned the game on the New Haven, Connecticut, campus after a series of injuries in 1982.

Although the game withered, the ball lives on in the form of the *cage ball*. A sphere produced in sizes up to 6 feet in diameter, the cage ball is a somewhat different beast than the pushball. It has a nylon shell and is typically replete with eight panels of various colors—a far cry from the tanned leather appearance of the pushball. Still, it is typically pushed around in games similar to those practiced with the pushball, albeit with one major difference: There's a lot less violence as elementary school kids represent the cage ball's primary market.

STATS AND FACTS

Dimensions: The pushball was typically 6 feet in diameter and weighed 50 pounds; the cage ball is the same size, but tends to weigh less.

Pushball by Horse: While the on-foot version of pushball is moribund, an equine style of the game still exists in Europe. Of course, a key issue is finding balls that will not burst when the horses trample on them.

Language: The phrase *stealing the ball* had special meaning in the early years of the game. Described as a "sensational" play by a 1905 issue of *National Magazine*, the maneuver involved eight members of one team forming a box and tackling the entire eleven-man opposing squad. This allowed the three remaining players to break away with the ball.

Racquetball

Joseph Sobek may be the unluckiest man in the ball world. Yet strangely, it never seemed to bother him. Sobek was a former tennis and squash pro who took a desk job at a

Bridgeport, Connecticut, rubber manufacturing plant in 1950—a great place to be if you want to invent a new ball. After spending so many years on the court, Sobek now began to see his waistline expand as his new position forced him to sit all day long on his "fanny" (his word, not mine). So he decided there needed to be an indoor sport just rigorous enough for the white-collar professional. Apparently handball was too strenuous and paddle tennis too sedate.

His invention was racquetball and he worked tirelessly at it. While making special racquets for the game—which he called paddle racquets—was important, he used his relationships in the rubber industry to perfect the ball. Sobek started with the inner core of a tennis ball like a Spaldeen-esque sphere (see page 121), but quickly moved on, toiling with engineers to come up with the right combination of bounce and resiliency. The hollow rubber ball needed to be softer than a handball but not as lively. A company called Seamco came through and the racquetball was born. Sobek saw the sphere as a masterstroke. "When you hit the ball, it makes an awful pop, and that's just a very satisfying noise," he said.

To tout his new ball and game, he hit the road promoting it at YMCAs across the country. Interestingly, he never competed in a tournament as Sobek's previous experience as a tennis professional made him ineligible to play in all-amateur tournaments hosted by the YMCA. By the late 1960s, hordes of aspiring yuppies saw racquetball as the perfect fitness activity. With the sport growing, Sobek handed off development of the game to experienced administrators.

From a financial standpoint, his timing couldn't have been worse. Within a decade of Sobek's official departure, racquetball became a colossal business. Companies like Colgate-Palmolive and Time Inc. were investing in the game, and manufacturers actually struggled to meet the demand for racquetballs. In 1977, players snapped up 14 million Seamco raquetballs—an amazing number considering the company had sold only 300,000 seven years earlier. Not only were Seamco and other companies selling in volume, they were also dishing out these balls at a premium price. The *Wall Street Journal* reported in 1978 that equipment makers were selling balls that cost 60 cents for $1.75. The normally capitalistic *Journal* aired claims by some that profits on the balls were "unseemly."

People were absolutely making money. But that group didn't include Sobek. He quietly returned to working as a tennis pro in Connecticut and never complained that the sport (or ball) he invented passed him by. "I'm just proud that something I started has become a multimillion-dollar sport played around the world," he mused.

STATS AND FACTS

Dimensions: The ball is 2.25 inches in diameter and weighs approximately 1.4 ounces.

Variation: In 1976, a British version of the game was introduced called *racketball* (ahh, what a difference two letters make). Along with modified rules, this variation uses a smaller, less dynamic ball.

Language: When a player gets a shot at a ball at the perfect height and depth, the ball is described as being in the *joy zone*. Some also describe this as *when the ball falls into your bucket*.

Red playground ball (cherry ball, red utility ball)

Envision an elementary school playground. It's nearly impossible to imagine kids running around on its blacktop surface without the sight of large red inflatable spheres being flung or kicked around. Classic childhood games such as *kickball*, *dodgeball*, and *four square* are the domain of the *playground ball*—colloquially known as the *cherry ball* or *utility ball* in some parts. Undoubtedly, the sturdy sphere has left an indelible mark (both literally and figuratively) on so many people. Nevertheless, it is actually a relatively new phenomenon.

The popular recess projectile appears to date back only to the late 1940s or early 1950s. Voit, a leading ball manufacturing company, began offering the red playground ball in the years following World War II. Why red? The pigment remained consistent even after taking a pounding on the blacktop, and like red bricks, it held up well in the sun. Ads heralding the all-purpose orb began appearing by 1947. Less than a decade later, the ball was everywhere. A 1953 *Los Angeles Times* article lamented how pastimes like *king of the mountain* and *duck on a rock* were being replaced by games that "[n]early all feature the use of a large, soccer-sized ball which can be kicked, thrown, bounced and rolled by youngsters all the way from first graders on up to eighth."

It's not that these games weren't being played before the playground ball was introduced. Dodgeball dates back to at least the first decade of the twentieth century. In a sign of those times, hard basketballs were used in the early days to pelt opponents according to one 1909 rules book. (A lighter, smaller sphere called a *gas ball* was appropriate in classrooms to protect the school's property. Phew!) Kickball references can also be found in the 1910s with a soccer ball or basketball serving as the forerunner to the playground ball. Games such as four square—in which competitors bounce a ball between marked-off squares—were also played.

But the red ball allowed for versatility. With one sphere, a group of kids could seamlessly switch from one game to another on a whim and the soft rubbery surface made it less dangerous than smacking kids with a basketball. Sadly, the picture of the school bell ringing and the all-purpose red ball flying may soon be a faded memory. Increasingly, companies are producing game-specific balls. One dodgeball, for example, is now covered with fabric to further diminish the sting of the ball. The worst part of it for nostalgia buffs: These spheres now come in all colors.

STATS AND FACTS

Dimensions: A typical utility ball is about 8.5 inches in diameter and weights between 11.6 and 13.3 ounces. One adult kickball organization (the World Adult Kickball Association) insists on a larger 10-inch ball, while a dodgeball sometimes comes in at a slightly smaller 8 inches.

Language: Variations on dodgeball include such dangerous-sounding games as *bombardment*, *prison ball*, *medic*, and *every man for himself*.

BALLS FOR SALE

Call it nostalgia or just a keen investment in history. Balls with some historical significance often sell well whether it be online or at auction. It seems that most sports have some special spheres worthy of purchase. Some examples:

1. A feathery golf ball made circa 1840 sold under the hammer for nearly £20,000 (approximately $32,000) in 1995.
2. The soccer ball English star Geoff Hurst used to score a hat trick in the 1966 World Cup finals (won by England) was bought in 1996 by the *Daily Mirror* newspaper from a former German player for a reported £70,000 pounds (approximately $105,700) in charity donations.
3. An original (large) "1965 Atom Logo" Wham-O Super Ball (in red, blue, or multicolor) can be found for sale online for $25 (original price: 99 cents).
4. An American transitional Leighton Oxblood marble dated between 1880 and 1910 goes for $1,200 to $2,000.
5. "Wilson"—the volleyball used in the Tom Hanks film *Cast Away*—was auctioned off for $18,400 in 2001. (It was actually one of three Wilsons used in the movie.)
6. Mark McGwire's seventieth home run baseball from the 1998 season was purchased by comic book creator Todd McFarlane for $3.045 million. At the time, the ball represented the single-year record for

---

Roulette ball

The odds of nailing down the true origins of roulette are about as likely as a casino losing money on this game of chance. Some claim that Romans invented it by spinning chariot wheels, while others believe French Dominican

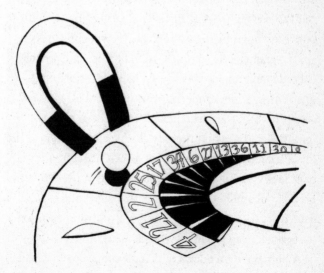

monks brought the game to Europe after seeing something similar played in China.

Yet even if either of these stories is true, it is unlikely that the little ball that we all follow so intently on the wheel was a part of the gambling process. The ball, which has unclear origins itself, likely found its way into the equation in the mid-seventeenth century. Credit for the modern roulette wheel design is generally attributed to famed French mathematician and physicist Blaise Pascal. Although he is best known for his contributions to geometry and probability theory, Pascal produced what is considered the roulette wheel's prototype while working on theories of perpetual motion—a concept, later debunked, that suggested a machine could be created that produced more energy than it consumed.

Pascal's wheel may have been a failure in thermodynamics, but seven decades later gamblers figured out it could make a fantastic betting device. The English used a wheel and ball for games called *roly-poly* and *even-odd*. But the serious-minded British put various bans on those pastimes, opening the way for the freewheeling French to get the game really spinning. In the 1790s, *roulette* (which is French for "small wheel") officially emerged and developed into its modern form over the next half-century. It seems certain that even before the modern roulette system, the ball circling the wheel was made of ivory. The material culled from elephant tusks was already very popular with billiard ball makers and proved to be a perfect substance for roulette. Its weight and elasticity gave ivory just the right amount of lively bounce when it descended from the upper wheel.

Albert Einstein once said, "You cannot beat a roulette

table unless you steal money from it." Seeing as Einstein was a pretty good mathematician, it's hard to argue otherwise. Not surprisingly, over the years, those looking to win at roulette through stealing have generally focused on the ball for help. In the nineteenth century, doctoring the roulette ball to increase the odds of succeeding was a legitimate concern. As if odds against the gamblers were not bad enough (the natural house advantage is more than 5 percent), much of this cheating was committed by the casinos. A roulette table would have electromagnets hidden inside the wheel and the ball would be fitted with a small iron core. The croupier, seeing the spread of bets on the table, pressed a button to magnetize part of the table and send the ball to a location where few had bet.

With the legalization of gambling in Nevada in 1931, government oversight meant that tricky roulette balls left respectable establishments. Nevertheless, enterprising scammers have not forgotten the value of the metal-cored roulette ball. In 1977, one man claimed he successfully manipulated the ball at a club in London. He allegedly swapped out a normal roulette ball for one with a metal center. He then used a magnet hidden in a lady's purse to manipulate the path of the ball. Whether this story is apocryphal or not, the real thing did happen in an Austrian casino in 2003. A five-person team got a metal core ball into a game and then used a device to move the ball within three spaces of their intended target. During several weeks they earned approximately £250,000 ($400,000). They were caught only after the ball stuck to a dealer's cuff links. Concerned casino owners now take precautions against these magic spheres by switching out balls, keeping a magnet near the table to check for metal cores, or even purchasing machines to prevent the use of electromagnetic fields on the gambling floor.

All this hasn't prevented the truly ambitious from cashing in. In 2004, three grifters scored £1.3 million (about $2.3 million) from a London casino without even tampering with the ball. Instead, they used computers to figure out roughly where the ball would land. With some knowledge of the characteristics of the ball and wheel—like the mass and size of the ball, the shape of the track, and the tilt of the wheel—they increase their odds from 37–1 to 6–1.

In true James Bond style, the criminals, some believe, used a laser scanner built into a mobile phone to calculate the velocity of the roulette ball and the speed of the wheel. As betters can place wagers after the ball has begun spinning, the crooks had just enough time to get their chips on the table. No doubt, Pascal would have been proud—of the math part at least.

STATS AND FACTS

Dimensions: In the United States, the ball is between 0.75 inch and 0.875 inch in diameter. It usually weighs around 1.6 ounces. European balls are smaller.

Strange But True: In 2004, a British man named Ashley Revell wagered his entire life savings—$135,300—on the spin of a roulette ball at the Plaza Hotel in Las Vegas. He correctly bet on red and doubled his money.

Language: *Ball tripping* is a way of cheating in which a little hole is drilled in the upper track where the ball is initially spun. The croupier will then hit a button that sends a ball toward the wheel prematurely. A good dealer can control the outcome of the spin with this maneuver.

Rugby ball

As the name would suggest, the sport originated at the Rugby School in the central English town of the same name. The myth is that a student named William Webb Ellis simply picked up a soccer ball one day and ran with

it, getting the game going in the 1820s. While this story is unlikely to be true, rugby became a favorite among the kids within the next decade, and two entrepreneurial cobblers stepped up to produce the necessary balls.

William Gilbert and Richard Lindon had shops right next to the Rugby School, and both offered leather rugby balls to the students. The originals were big and a little more oblong than previous orbs used for soccer-like kicking games (though some have described them as plum shaped). There was probably enough business for both men because the rugby ball took a lot of time and effort to construct. Each one was different because its characteristics were primarily defined by the shape of the leather-encased pig's bladder the artisans used to craft each ball.

One element that distinguished a good ball from an inferior model was getting proper air pressure in the final product. As a result, producing the best ball required more than fine leather and deft handiwork with a needle—it necessitated a really good set of lungs. In the days before the hand-operated pumps, a clay straw was used to manually blow up the balls. This was a job that required both lung power and willpower because many of the pig bladders were diseased and in a horrible-smelling "green state."

It was this element that gave Gilbert the advantage over his competitor, Lindon. By the 1850s, Gilbert had a secret weapon: his golden-lunged nephew James Gilbert. James was such a rock star that one source gushed he was ". . . a wonder of lung strength and blew even the big match balls up tight." Whom did Lindon give the gig to in his shop? His wife. Yep, the dutiful Mrs. Lindon was responsible for filling the bladders. But the work wore on the fair lady, and after years on the job, she contracted lung disease—likely from handling the diseased bladders—and died.

One would think his wife's tragic death might have deterred Lindon, but it actually inspired him. With the invention of vulcanized rubber, Lindon came up with a rubber alternative to the pig's bladder. He also devised a brass hand pump so nobody would have to suffer his spouse's terrible fate. Unfortunately for Lindon, he wasn't the best at calculating and neglected to patent his inventions. The Gilbert clan picked up on the rubber bladder and it became the industry norm (much to the relief of pigs everywhere).

With the new materials, the design could be standardized. The oval became the shape of choice. These first rubber bladder balls looked a bit like little watermelons or, as one contemporary song put it, an "outgrown egg." Realizing that carrying a watermelon was a bit much, players pressured organizers to shrink the size, and over time it became smaller and sleeker (though never as pointy as American football).

Adroit businessmen, the Gilberts opened up the mail-order market to keen players in Australia and New Zealand and ultimately dominated the industry. Although the family sold the business in 1978, the company and others have continued to tweak the ball by mainly updating the outer shell with high-tech materials and new panel configurations.

STATS AND FACTS

Dimensions: The Rugby Union ball is approximately 11 to 11.8 inches long, and its circumference is about 23 inches. It weighs between 14.5 and a little more than 16 ounces.

Variation: When most Americans think of rugby, they are probably picturing Rugby *Union*. In the late nineteenth century an alternative code was developed in

England's North called Rugby *League*, which remains popular in that region as well as in parts of Australia and New Zealand. The ball in League play tends to be slightly smaller and lighter.

Strange But True: The inside lining of nineteenth-century rugby balls came from the same place as one of the world's most popular raincoats. Charles Macintosh invented both the first waterproof cloth raincoat (aka the Mackintosh) and supplied the rubber bladders for early rugby balls.

Language: A *dummy* can sometimes be the smartest play in rugby. The term is used for faking a pass. A *dummy-half* is also a term for a position in Rugby League.

Shot put

Chucking the shot put is the ultimate competition of human versus ball. There are no walls to hit or nets to clear or bats to swing or gloves to catch. It's just one person trying to launch a heavy orb as far as possible.

Although Homer makes mention of rock-throwing competitions by soldiers during the siege of Troy, the shot put was surprisingly not an event at the ancient Olympics held by the Greeks. The discus was the projectile of choice for those athletes. Instead, hurling a ball for sport got its start in Scotland. It's said that throwing the *clachneart*— a rock larger and slightly heavier than the modern shot put—dates back 2,000 years in the Highlands, where stone heaving is still a big part of local competitions.

The English also have a long history of throwing boulders. In the twelfth century, a monk named William Fitzstephen wrote about land being set aside near London for kids to practice, among other sports, "casting of the

stone." Launching big rocks became so popular that in 1365 Edward III put it on a list of prohibited sports so the country's young men could properly focus on the more important skill of archery. Although the restriction lasted for centuries, it doesn't appear that it applied to royalty. The famed Henry VIII enjoyed casting the stone and throwing a heavy ball attached to a cord about 150 years after Edward's edict.

Over time, the stones gave way to iron spheres. These early balls were shot or, more specifically, cannonballs. Early *round shot* was generally made of stone because of the high cost of metal. But beginning in the 1600s, iron balls became the common substance for artillery ammunition, leading British military personnel to begin throwing heavy metal instead of stone spheres. Formalized rules were set in 1860 with a 16-pound ball being the standard weight for official international men's competitions (the women's shot is a little more than half that weight). Because of the ball's weight, participants were prohibited from throwing with a bent arm (it was considered too dangerous) and were required to keep the ball in the crook of the neck before releasing. The event became a regular part of track and field competitions, and despite being snubbed by the ancient Greeks, the shot put was included at the first modern Olympic Games in 1896.

While the weight of the spheres is etched in stone, those tussling with the heavy ball do have some flexibility when it comes to picking which orb to toss. In international competition, shot puts are made of either brass or iron. Stainless steel is also allowed under some circumstances as are balls with polyurethane covers. (The key: The shot put's surface must be smooth.) Competitors are allowed some leeway in size as well. Balls are about the dimension of a grapefruit but can vary almost 1 inch in diameter. This allows competitors to get just the right feel.

Getting the right attitude is equally important. Parry O'Brien, who won two Olympic shot put gold medals in the 1950s, believed that a little anger helped make him a champion. "You've got to be mentally ready to make the toss," O'Brien once said. "You've got to get nervous, get your blood flowing hot. You've got to get your metabolism going faster and faster. Your heart has got to go like a trip-hammer. I try to whip myself into a frenzy. When I'm ready for a toss, I'm in a different world."

Dimensions: The men's ball can be between 4.33 and 5.12 inches in diameter, and the women's ranges from 3.74 to 4.33 inches. The men's ball weighs 16 pounds and the women's 8.8 pounds.

Variation: When the shot put is attached to a steel cord with a rigid handle at the end, it's referred to as the *hammer*. The hammer throw is also an Olympic sport.

Strange But True: For some, throwing the shot put just isn't enough. Records have been established for tossing a variety of other unexpected items, including frozen whole tuna (more than 122 feet), cow dung (182.3 feet), a rolling pin (175.42 feet), and a cell phone (more than 314 feet). For the record, the longest shot put throw is 75 feet, 10 inches.

Language: The *glide* and the *spin* are two techniques for throwing the shot put. The glide, which is typically for beginners, requires sidestepping up to a designated line before heaving the shot put; the more advanced spin involves starting backward and then spinning 180 degrees to the front of the circle before releasing.

Sliotar

Rule number one of ball making: Give yourself a competitive advantage if you're ever going to use the ball you've created. Ned Treston must have missed class that day.

Treston was from the Irish hamlet of Gort in South Galway and in 1886 was selected to play in a hurling match against North Tipperary. Hurling is a rough sport

dating back centuries. The game features players each armed with a short curved stick, known as a *hurley*, primarily hacking at each other—although the actual objective is to smack a ball, called the *sliotar*, past a keeper into an opposing team's goal. On this February day in Dublin, both parties brought their own sliotar but neither would agree to use the other team's ball.

A leatherworker by trade, Treston left the field and went to a saddle maker near Dublin Castle, where he constructed a sliotar that both teams could live with. Treston is remembered—particularly in his hometown of Gort—as creating the prototype of the modern sliotar. What he cannot be remembered for from that day is being a winner, as despite making the ball, his South Galway team lost to North Tipperary 1–0.

While Treston might get some contemporary credit in the sliotar's development, this ball is the stuff of legends. In fact, the sphere plays prominently in one of the most popular Celtic fables, *The Legend of Cu Cahlainn*. In the tale a young hero named Setanta expertly plays hurling with a silver sliotar and, according to some versions of the story, uses a ball to slay a vicious dog. Other lore claims that Celtic invaders defeated the island's natives in a game of hurling to earn dominion over Ireland. Even the etymology of the word *sliotar* has an epic feel. Most experts believe it comes from the combination of the Irish *sliabh* (mountain) and *thar* (across).

Unlike Setanta's precious ball, most early sliotars were made of simpler stuff. A wooden-cored ball wrapped in rope and leather was most common—although bronze was sometimes noted as an element used in making the orb. Of course, the problem with this ball was it was very heavy. Throw in Ireland's wet weather and the porous sphere also ended up exceedingly soggy.

Along with Treston, a hurling player from Bruff, County Limerick, named Johnny McAuliffe was a key sliotar innovator. In the early twentieth century, he substituted the wood center with a cork core to give the ball more bounce. He also replaced the quickly soaked brown leather outer shell with a white tanned pigskin cover, making it easier to follow and more durable in the rain. Equally important, McAuliffe invented a lip running at the seams of the ball (think of a soft-ish baseball with big ridges). This was important because when you're trying to balance the sliotar on your hurley (a legal maneuver for up to four steps), any advantage like the lip is helpful. McAuliffe's version was such a hit that it became the standard ball.

To this day, the Irish take the sliotar very seriously. In 2006, a fight broke out when a County Cork player tried to sneak one unsanctioned brand of ball onto the field in an important game. Disagreement may occur about the composition of the ball, but few in Ireland will dispute where the sacred sliotar should come from—the Emerald Isle. In fact, the sport's governing body, the Gaelic Athletic Association (GAA), has rules insisting that balls be produced by the Irish industry. Alas, in 2008, it was revealed that many of the Irish sliotars were imported from such locales as Pakistan and China. "We live in the real world, times change. . . . Most of manufacturing has migrated abroad," lamented GAA director Pat Daly. In a touch of irony, Daly made his comments from the organization's Croke Park headquarters in Dublin—just 6 miles east of where Treston introduced his ball more than a century earlier.

STATS AND FACTS

Dimensions: Approximately 9 to 9.8 inches in circumference and weighing 3.9 to 4.2 ounces.

Variations: Along with hurling, the sliotar is used in a women's variation of the sport called *carmogie* (slightly smaller ball). The Scottish sport of *shinty* (a little more similar in rules to field hockey) uses a ball similar in design to the sliotar but smaller and lighter (7.5 to 8 inches in circumference and weighing 2.5 to 3 ounces).

Language: Although the sport is simply called hurling today, it was actually known in the eighteenth century as *hurling at goals*. Another version of hurling features whole villages pitted in an all-out battle over several square miles.

Soccer ball

Soccer is known throughout most of the world as "the beautiful game," but its origins and early balls were far from pretty. Though the Chinese were kicking around balls

more than 2,000 years ago, the sport as we know it came from mob rules games in the British Isles beginning about 1,000 years later. These *folk* or *festival football* contests (see page 4) were played over expansive fields and pitted hundreds against each other in no-rules mayhem. The game was so consuming (and dangerous) that various kings and municipalities banned the sport over the years.

While the British referred to the ball as a *football*, it didn't mean that every game used the feet. Some scholars suggest the term merely indicated that the sport was played on foot rather than on horseback. If true, it seems that the horseball or hoofball never caught on (though polo did). According to another source, the name was more aspirational. Locals used the term because the ball *could* be kicked as it was the proper size and it bounced the right amount to be played off the foot. Whatever the origin, legend adds a lot of color to the items that villagers decided fit the definition of a football. These included inflated pig, sheep, and cow bladders; stitched-up balls of cloth; and even skulls and human heads. (Who knew there was that much bounce in a skull?)

As the game moved from a mini-military skirmish to a more contained competition on a field with goals and a limited number of players, a pig's bladder encased in leather became the norm. Still, standardization didn't initially bother organizers. The English Football Association was formed in 1863, but the original rules made no mention of what the ball should look like. It took nine years of kicking around various odd-sized balls before somebody figured it would be nice to get everybody on the same page in terms of the dimensions. It then took even longer before deciding on a universal weight.

That said, at the time, setting a specific weight was almost academic. Although durable rubber had replaced the pig's bladder for the ball's insides, the leather casing, which was laced together, easily became waterlogged on wet British turf. The result was a ball that was as heavy as a rock. Try heading a rock on a cold English day; one can only presume it's not a great feeling. But that didn't stop intrepid players from banging balls off their noggins well into the late twentieth century. (In recent years, some scientists have tied this practice to dementia in older soccer players.)

As Dustin Hoffman learned in *The Graduate*, players must give praise to the powers that be for plastics. This led the way to waterproofing in the 1970s, which diminished head trauma. The ball also got a makeover during this period. R. Buckminster Fuller was an American architect who influenced the look of the soccer ball more than any individual (fancy a Yank revolutionizing the world's game!). Fuller, who is best known for popularizing the geodesic dome, also came up with a design of twenty hexagonal and twelve pentagonal pieces that, when sewn together, made a near perfect sphere. His actual goal was not sports-oriented—he wanted to come up with a design that required the least amount of materials. Nevertheless, the *Buckyball* became a soccer standard for decades.

Today, the Buckyball is no longer the chosen design for world-class soccer. Because the sport is such big business, the race to develop a newer, greater, more high-tech (insert more superlatives here) ball is never-ending. Current high-end spheres are no longer hand-sewn but are glued together with the help of thermal technology. A microtextured synthetic surface is said to prevent hydroplaning when the shoe hits the ball. This isn't always a good thing: New balls introduced for the World Cup over the past decade have been roundly criticized by players, who disdain the slick new materials or say the ball's trajectory has been oddly altered. Still, progress moves on. There are even cutting-edge microchips that can let you know whether a ball has crossed the goal line. Try putting that in a skull.

STATS AND FACTS

Dimensions: The dimensions haven't changed much in more than a century—the circumference must be about 27 to 28 inches and it should weigh around 14 to 16 ounces.

Strange But True: Some historians claim that Mary Queen of Scots refereed one of the earliest modern-style soccer games. While confined at Carlisle Castle in Scotland in 1568, she supposedly tossed a leather ball from her window and oversaw a ten-on-ten contest between Scottish and French courtiers. While no score was kept, records said that the ball figured heavily in the match. According to the Calendar of Scottish Papers, "her retinue played at football before her, very strongly, nimbly and skillfully, without foul play—the smallness of theyr balle occasioning their fairer play."

Quality Control: In 1946, the Football Association (FA) Cup Final, which is English soccer's crown jewel event, was marred by a bad ball. In a tight 1–1 match between Derby County and Charlton Athletic, the game ball burst midkick near the end of regulation play. Red-faced officials replaced the defective sphere and Derby took advantage, scoring three goals in overtime to seal the victory 4–1. Shockingly, a ball popped again the following year. Organizers attributed the embarrassing balls to poor post–World War II materials.

Language: To distinguish their sport from other forms of football (such as rugby), nineteenth-century soccer organizers called the game *association football*. The word *soccer* is said to be an abbreviated slang term that comes from "association."

Softball

Softball players around the world owe a debt of gratitude to the sport of boxing. The reason: A glove used for the sweet science of pugilism provided the beginnings of

the softball. The origins of the ball date back to a frigid Thanksgiving afternoon in 1887 in Chicago. A group of about twenty young men were nervously waiting for the score of the Harvard-Yale football game at the Gothic-looking Farragut Boathouse just off Lake Michigan.

When the score came in—Yale 17, Harvard 8—the fellas got a little rowdy. One Yale supporter picked up an old boxing glove and threw it at a Harvard man. Seeing the projectile coming, the man grabbed a broom handle and swatted the glove back over the Yalie's head. Although Harvard and Yale have approximately sixty graduates who have earned Nobel Prizes, what happened next should have earned some sort of prize from the sports world.

George W. Hancock, a reporter for the Chicago Board of Trade, suggested they start playing ball. The boxing glove was tied tightly into a ball using its laces, a bat was fashioned from the broom handle, and a makeshift diamond was mapped out with chalk. Hancock liked what he saw, and when the frivolities came to an end, he began hatching a plan of great ambition.

The next week Hancock formulated the new game. A man of letters rather than of trade, he subcontracted the work on the ball. According to the *1903 Indoor Base Ball Guide*, Hancock "directed Augustus J. White on how to make a ball which could be seen at night and fill the requirements of the game." The details of that sphere aren't clear, but it must have worked, as the sport spread quickly throughout Chicago that winter.

Within two years of the inaugural contest, Hancock had published rules for what he dubbed "Indoor Base Ball." At the time, his requirements for the game balls were pretty simple, but years later he would offer a more explicit blueprint of the early softball. An appropriate ball had a "core made up of packed leather scraps around which is placed curled horsehair, tied on with string," he wrote in the *Los Angeles Times* in 1903. "The cover is a softer horsehide than that used on the outdoor ball, but made in the same manner as regards to shape of flaps and sewing."

Hancock deserves tremendous credit for apostle-like zeal at pushing his game. But the idea of modifying softball for the outdoors was not really his own. Other versions of the game were popping up all across the United States in places such as Minneapolis, where an outdoor version was played by firefighters under the surprisingly unmanly name of *kitten ball*. Other variations included *playground ball*, *diamond ball*, and *serve us ball*, and each had their own ball, ranging from ones just larger than a baseball to melon-sized spheres. All these games did have one thing in common: They were all modified, often easier to play, reworkings of baseball, which by this time was quickly becoming America's most popular pastime.

Nevertheless, even these more casual versions of baseball required some standardization, and the 1933 World's Fair in Chicago provided a venue for it. The event's theme was "A Century of Progress" and it featured countries from all around the world displaying various aspects of their culture. When it came to highlighting U.S. customs, *Chicago American* journalist Leo Fischer and local sporting goods dealer M. J. Pauley figured softball was as good a choice as any and proposed a tournament to the organizers. That they chose the sobriquet *softball* to describe the game was a big decision in and of itself. The term had only been created earlier that year (presumably to indicate the game was a relatively gentle form of baseball since the ball itself was getting pretty hard by this point); we could just as well all be playing Kitten Ball in our corporate leagues had things turned out differently. Even with a singular name, there was still disarray within the sport. Fifty-five teams were invited to play at the 1933 World's Fair and they all probably played by different rules—and with a different ball—before attending. The tournament did ultimately use a variety of rules (there were slow-pitch and fast-pitch events), but one element was universal: The games all featured a 14-inch-circumference ball.

Using the same-sized ball and consistent rules were important, but there was another central development during the Depression that spurred softball. The outdoor game was extremely popular in urban areas because the sport, unlike baseball, could be played in the tight space constraints of big cities. The problem was that on asphalt and concrete, the balls were getting ripped apart too quickly. For most people in these economically bereft times, it was too costly to replace a damaged ball. Frederick deBeer recognized this problem, and in 1934 he patented a softball called the "Clincher." This innovative ball featured seams sewn underneath the outer shell of the sphere. The unique design prevented the stitching from hitting against the tough ground and splitting. Although other companies such as Spalding had their own version of the protected seam, deBeer's ball became a favorite in New York City and Chicago, helping grow the game in key markets by cutting costs on new equipment. To this day, the 16-inch version of the Clincher—known also as a "mushball"—is de rigueur in the Windy City.

Over the years, the size of the ball elsewhere was set at 12 inches for both the fast-pitch and the slow-pitch games. Though the circumference is standard, it hasn't prevented sporting goods manufacturers from tinkering with the ball's insides in an effort to make it fly farther. The problem: These balls proved *too* powerful, especially when they came in contact with increasingly more technologically impressive bats. Still, the softball world is pretty happy with its options nowadays. As was the case with that boxing glove first used by inventor George Hancock and his friends, the key is simply finding the ball that packs just the right punch.

STATS AND FACTS

Dimensions: A circumference of 11.875 to 12.25 inches and a weight of 6.25 to 7 ounces.

Baseball Difference: A baseball is approximately 3 inches smaller in circumference, weighs 1 to 2 ounces less, and has 20 more red stitches on the outside (108 compared with the 88 on a softball).

Speed Ball: Fast-pitch softball pitchers have proved their ability on more than one occasion against Major League Baseball superstars. Babe Ruth reportedly struck out on three straight pitches in softball games in both 1937 and 1938. In 1962, Joan Joyce, a highly acclaimed female hurler, faced off against Ted Williams. The Red Sox great got forty pitches and only made contact twice— getting one hit and fouling another ball off.

Language: Though the game is called softball, the hardness of the orb is actually very important. The term *COR* refers to the *coefficient of restitution* of a softball. The ball must have just the right firmness so as not to be too soft or too rigid.

Space Hopper (Hopper, Ride-a-Roo, Kangaroo Ball, Hoppity Hop)

In the late 1960s and early 1970s, one of the battlefields for the hearts and minds of children in the United States and Great Britain was atop a big bouncing ball. Sold under such

names as the *Space Hopper*, the *Hopper*, the *Ride-a-Roo*, the *Kangaroo Ball*, and the *Hoppity Hop*, these polyvinyl orbs offered hours of fun for kids, who bounced on them clutching two ribbed "horns" or some other form of handle.

This was big business. Sun Products Corp. produced the Hoppity Hop and its strategy was to bombard the airwaves and newspapers. Starting with its introduction in 1968 until the mid-1970s, the Hoppity Hop was ubiquitous on television. In newspapers from Bowling Green, Kentucky, to Los Angeles, California, Hoppity Hop ads proudly announced, "AS SEEN ON TV." So much was invested in marketing that when Sun moved the Hoppity Hop campaign from one ad agency to another, the winners of the account boasted to the *New York Times* that it was a "million dollar client"—a serious amount of cash in the early 1970s.

Other companies looked to endorsements when pushing their version of the ball. In 1968, the year the ball came to America from Europe, the makers of the Kangaroo Ball sponsored famed bowler LaVerne Carter, who was one of America's top female players. As part of the deal, Carter traveled town-to-town for tour events with three balls—two for bowling and one for bouncing. When she did an interview with the *Miami Herald*, Carter answered questions while hopping on a Kangaroo Ball.

In England, the Ride-a-Roo had its own celebrity support. In January 1968, Emanuel Shinwell, an eighty-three-year-old Baron who served as a cabinet head in Prime Minister Clement Atlee's administration, agreed to bound around on the ball for a photo opportunity. A more athletic Lillian Bond, who would win a silver medal in the 400 meters at the Mexico City Olympic Games that summer, paid respect to the ball after using it. "It does take a fair amount of lung power to keep it going. I mean, you've really got to make your legs work at it," she admitted. The attention surely helped the Ride-a-Roo become a hit, as evidenced by the fact that it spawned a novelty song in 1968. "Ride-a-Roo" by Teresa Brewer talked about the fun of going "jumpity jump" on the ball and made reference to its popularity in England.

The reason for the heavy competition was the balls didn't have a single uniform design. Aquilino Cosani, a plastics maker from Italy who'd previously created the exercise ball (see page 46), is generally credited with developing the ball. In 1968, he patented a handle for the big sphere. But others were also devising their own blueprints, such as two British inventors who patented their own "ridable bouncing ball recreational device" the same year.

While the balls lost their spring in the marketplace by the 1980s, they are still for sale on both sides of the Atlantic. A number of the original spheres sported the caricature of a kangaroo's face on the front of the hopper. (Ball colors varied, but the first balls in the United Kingdom tended to be orange; the American versions were normally red, yellow, or blue.) In the years since, many famous icons have graced the front of these balls. They've included Mickey Mouse, Donald Duck, Barbie, and Thomas the Tank Engine. That's a pretty impressive roster for a ball that once relied on a bouncing bowler for attention.

STATS AND FACTS

DIMENSIONS: Balls range in diameter from 1.3 feet for small children to 2.6 feet for adults. A 24-inch ball can weigh almost 4 pounds.

Language: Some other names for the ball have included *skippy ball*, *PON-PON*, *bouncy ball*, and *kangaroo jockey ball*.

QUOTING BALLS

For centuries, the ball has been a go-to object for authors looking to make statements about our world. Some take it as a metaphor and others just use it to make a point. The following five powerful thinkers are among the many who have played with the ball:

Happiness is a ball after which we run wherever it rolls, and we push it with our feet when it stops.
—GERMAN WRITER JOHANN WOLFGANG VON GOETHE

Thus so wretched is man that he would weary even without any cause for weariness . . . and so frivolous is he that, though full of a thousand reasons for weariness, the least thing, such as playing billiards or hitting a ball, is sufficient enough to amuse him.
—FRENCH MATHEMATICIAN AND PHILOSOPHER BLAISE PASCAL

The clock struck nine when I did send the nurse. . . . Had she affections and warm youthful blood, She would be as swift in motion as a ball; My words would bandy her to my sweet love.
—BRITISH POET WILLIAM SHAKESPEARE (JULIET FROM *ROMEO AND JULIET*)

It is a noteworthy fact that kicking and beating have played so considerable a part in the habits which necessity has imposed on mankind in past ages that the only way of preventing civilized men from beating and kicking their wives is to organize games in which they can kick and beat balls.
—BRITISH AUTHOR GEORGE BERNARD SHAW

Truth is tough. It will not break, like a bubble, at a touch; nay, you may kick it about all day, like a football, and it will be round and full at the evening.
—AMERICAN JURIST OLIVER WENDELL HOLMES

Squash ball

Throughout the history of squash, creating consensus on the perfect ball has been elusive. Discussions, debates, and downright disagreements have swirled around the ball almost since its origin. Maybe this shouldn't be surprising as the sport was created by the elite of the upper class, who were accustomed to getting their own way.

Squash, which uses a smaller ball and is a more precise game than its younger cousin, racquetball, began in the mid-nineteenth century at Harrow, a British boarding school for the rich and privileged. The story goes that younger students waiting to get on courts for another smack-the-ball-against-the-wall competition called rackets came up with the new game. Left without the space necessary to play rackets, these impatient lads improvised, using confined areas near the popular courts. The upshot was they were forced to play by different rules and use smaller racquets and a softer ball that wouldn't bounce quite as far in their cramped space. The game quickly earned a following, but why it was called squash has elicited controversy. Many believe it comes from the sound the ball made when smacked against the wall. But squash expert James Zug disputes this explanation, asserting the sport's title relates to a Harrow hazing ritual of the time that was also called squash. Whatever the actual roots of the game's name, when rich people travel, they take their sports with them, and it didn't take long for the sport to migrate to the United States. At first, a squash-tennis hybrid, featuring a tennis ball, swept the United States. It was quickly embraced by privileged Yankees such as John D. Rockefeller Jr. and Jay Gould. But before long, Americans were playing with a squash-specific ball that was bigger, heavier, and faster than that of their counterparts across the sea. Numerous explanations were posited to rationalize the difference. One account explained that a British squash official was en route to the United States with the proper design for the ball and court (as the American courts were also smaller), but had the misfortune of sailing on the *Titanic* and perished. Another suggested that the larger U.S. ball was better in the bitter cold of New England, where squash's American roots were planted. A third claim was simply that Americans were stubborn and didn't want to play the British way.

Even within the United States, standardizing the ball continued to be "the most vexatious issue" deep into the twentieth century, according to Zug. The greatest debate stemmed from what element of the game the balls should emphasize. With slower balls, cardiovascular endurance was the key. Quite simply, the guy who could survive long rallies would likely win. With the faster balls, tactics such as positioning and ball placement were more important as one big hit could win the point. For the most part, the Americans stuck with speed. As if the consistency wasn't reason enough for debate, the color of the ball also led to disagreement in North America. Because the squash ball had a darkish hue, U.S. organizers required that courts be whitewashed to make it easier to see the ball. Canadians didn't understand the big deal and insisted that their courts keep a nice natural wood-stained finish. This rift took decades to settle (chalk one up for the Canadians as the United States eventually relaxed on the color scheme).

Matters were no better in Great Britain. In some instances, aristocratic eccentricities were in full effect when it came to ball preference. A Harrow alum named Vernon Harcourt built a squash court at his home in Oxford in 1883, and the choice of ball was a big concern. Rather than playability, the issue was aesthetics. At first they used a black ball, but dismayed with its markings, they changed to a red ball, which, according to Harcourt's son, "gave the walls a pleasant pink hue."

Squash elites will likely squabble over the perfect ball for eternity, but nowadays, technology has allowed players to tackle other concerns—such as making sure that the ball is properly warmed up. Cold squash balls just don't get the bounce that warmer versions get as a match develops (this is called *game heat*). As a result, the whole dynamic of the game can change if a ball splits in the middle of a tight contest and a new cold one is needed. Enter a modern marvel: Companies now sell squash ball warmers. Surely, arguments will one day rage over the best machine for this job.

STATS AND FACTS

Dimensions: Professional balls are 1.6 inches in diameter (give or take about 0.02 inch) and weigh about 0.85 ounce (with some slight deviation allowed). Balls are also judged on resiliency and seam strength.

Strange But True: In the mid-1980s two British dentists waged a legal war over the patent for a squash ball that could be easily followed on television. Bob Morris, the chief executive of the Squash Rackets Association, called the ball "a crucial breakthrough" for televising squash matches. The two men ended up splitting the patent, but even with Morris's breathless excitement, the sport never became a TV darling.

Language: A *dead nick* is considered the perfect shot. It occurs when a ball hits the wall and rolls flat across the floor, unplayable.

Stress ball

The stress ball is practically omnipresent. Go to any corporate confab and you're bound to get a squishy sphere emblazoned with a company logo in your goody bag. When the venerable Lehman Brothers went bankrupt, the investment bank had 2,055 stress balls as part of its last bits of assets.

Considering its ubiquity, it might be hard to imagine that the concept of the stress ball was conceived by one man. No doubt, people have been squeezing objects as a way to relieve anxiety throughout history, but Alex Carswell, a transplanted New Yorker living in Studio City, California, was the individual who coined the term *Stressball* in October 1988. His product was a blue, softball-sized Nerf-like ball equipped with a microchip that produced the sound of shattering glass when it hit something. Carswell said he invented the ball after throwing a pen at a wall in frustration. The projectile broke a picture of his mom, leading the inventor to create a less damaging alternative. "Maybe it'll make people laugh and they'll live a couple of years longer," Carswell said at the time.

Despite the creator's Zen aspirations, his device had its immediate detractors. In 1989, *Sports Illustrated* said the Stressball was "a little too big to fit in one hand, a little too hard to squeeze and just similar enough to Styrofoam to make you anxious about the ozone layer.... It is nothing more than a lowly descendant of fast-food containers, baseballs, and static-ridden walkie-talkies, desperately struggling to become a real ball." Ouch. Still, the ball did find a place in the sporting world—or more specifically, in the hands of flamboyant Dallas Cowboys All-Pro wide receiver Michael Irvin. Following a 1992 game against the Philadelphia Eagles, Irvin pulled out one of Carswell's toys while meeting with journalists. "It's my stress ball," Irvin told reporters. "Every time you ask a question that stresses me, it goes off." Before long, the sound of breaking glass filled the room.

The Stressball itself may not have resonated with everyone, but the idea certainly did. Within just a few years of its introduction, other companies began marketing their own version. In 1992, the National Exercise for Life Institute placed the ball on its top ten healthy gift guide list. Unlike Carswell's spongy concoction, these newer balls were made with a latex casing and a mushy viscoelastic polymer filler that offered more of a pleasing resistance to the hand. In 1994, a company called Pro-innovative released the Gripp as both a stress ball and a hand trainer. Constructed with four latex layers sealed around millet seeds, the ball earned multiple patents for its design. Other options emerged using latex exteriors but stuffed with everything from synthetic micro beads to oozy gels. Spongy polyurethane balls became particularly popular—though they often deviated from the traditional orb shape. Because they are molded from liquid, you can get these squeeze items in any shape imaginable. For the financially strapped (or those who don't go to too many corporate events), a stress reliever can be made right at home using a balloon and either sand or flour.

STATS AND FACTS

Dimensions: Stress balls tend to be approximately 2.25 inches in diameter and 3.5 ounces in weight. (Polyurethane types come in all shapes and sizes.)

Add-ons: Besides squeezability, some stress ball companies offer other bells and whistles. There are scented balls with such aromas as melon, mint, and pink grapefruit, and there are noisemakers. Instead of the original breaking glass, a hearty laugh is available with one ball.

Strange But True: The stress ball is not always used for good. In 2008, British MP George Galloway was pelted in the face by a pale blue stress ball while campaigning in London's Holborn area. Although Galloway was knocked down, the hit may have caused a bit of stress relief among locals. "Given the applause that reportedly echoed around Holborn following the hit, using the ball to vent anger clearly went down a bomb," the *Herald* of Glasgow, Scotland, claimed after the affair. Galloway was ultimately fine, and as for the culprit, he walked away with just a warning.

Language: *Sorbothane*, which was one of the first materials used inside stress balls, has a number of other applications beyond being enjoyable to grip. It has been used to cushion the Liberty Bell while being transported and to protect NASA cameras on the space shuttle *Discovery*.

SuperBall

Only a very special ball could serve as inspiration for one of the world's biggest sporting events without ever being used in that contest. In 1966, when professional

football was debating a name for its championship game, Kansas City Chiefs owner Lamar Hunt began thinking of his children playing with an ultra-springy SuperBall. Almost whimsically, Hunt threw out the title "Super

Bowl." The idea had the bounce of a lead weight, but it stuck.

"It was a name we all admitted was way too corny to be used—and that included [National Football League commissioner] Pete Rozelle," Hunt recalled years later. "But we all referred to it that way among ourselves, and the [TV] networks picked up on it."

In honor of that momentous event, a SuperBall even has a place in the Pro Football Hall of Fame in Canton, Ohio.

Not bad for a ball that almost never existed. Norman Stingley came up with the idea while working as a chemist for a rubber company in Whittier, California, in the mid-1960s. He began pressurizing synthetic rubber in his spare time and found that, when formed into a sphere, it had incredible bounce. He offered up the discovery to his bosses, but they weren't interested because the ball couldn't hold its shape and fell apart after just a few minutes. Undeterred, Stingley kept tinkering with his invention and moved on to Wham-O, a company famed for its kid-friendly handiwork such as the Frisbee and the Hula Hoop.

When Stingley entered the Wham-O offices in 1964 to meet the company owners, he lightly bounced the ball on the table and then handed it over to Wham-O cofounder Arthur "Spud" Melin. Not realizing the spring in the ball, Melin bounced it a little harder and the ball flew all the way to the ceiling. The Wham-O folks were impressed, but it was another trick that sealed the deal. Along with its incredible bounce, the ball also had amazing grip when it hit an object. With the right spin at the proper angle, a ball could be thrown under the table, hit it, and then fling back into the hand of the thrower. After seeing "the table trick," Wham-O was sold.

Still, the ball wasn't a certainty to make it to market because it just kept breaking apart. In the end (for you chemists at home), a synthetic rubber formula with additives of sulfur, zinc oxide, antioxidants, and colorants cooked for 15 to 20 minutes at 320 degrees Fahrenheit at 1,000 pounds per square inch did the trick. While the ball would still chip and break after wear, it now had acceptable resiliency. In his patent application, Stingley humbly claimed that "as an article of play, the eccentricity of reaction makes the ball a highly entertaining and amusing toy."

Once perfected, the marketing wizards at Wham-O took over. They dubbed it the *SuperBall* and changed the name of the material used for production from Stingley's scientific sounding *polybutadiene* to the more out-of-this-world term *Zectron*. The ball was also described in terms only a salesman could dream of. The box claimed the SuperBall was the "most fantastic ball ever created by science!" It also depicted the dark purple ball, which was about the size of a plum, taking one hop and leaping over a large family home. Offering a bit of a science-fair-project-gone-awry feel, it also stated, "It's almost alive!"

At 98 cents a unit, the SuperBall was a huge hit. About 6 million balls were reportedly sold when it debuted in 1965. Keen to capitalize on the SuperBall success, Wham-O developed numerous different-sized balls with the famed Zectron. These included a SuperBall baseball, a SuperBall golf ball, and SuperBall dice. The company even fashioned a SuperBall bowling ball for a promotional event. It was so powerful that it once bounded down a hotel hallway and broke through a wall.

As cheap pretenders flooded the market, the SuperBall's sales dipped so much that, in 1977, Wham-O ceased making them. Thankfully for nostalgia fiends everywhere, the ball returned in 1998 as the company, which is no longer owned by its original founders, recommitted to its traditional toys.

STATS AND FACTS

Dimensions: Though many different sizes were produced, the traditional ball is 1.9 inches in diameter and weighs 2.1 ounces.

Competitors: Though many no-name brands entered the market to compete with the SuperBall, the "Zoomball" was a top challenger. It claimed to have double the compressed energy as the SuperBall, which meant it could bound over a three-story building (compared to just the two-story suburban house illustrated on the SuperBall packaging). All this was offered for only 49 cents.

Work of Art: In 2004, the SuperBall was included at a New York Museum of Modern Art exhibit called "Humble Masterpieces." Along with the SuperBall were such everyday items as the Band-Aid, a white T-shirt, and the Post-it Note.

Language: *Ski-Hi* and *Jet Ball* were just two of the names used for Wham-O SuperBalls that featured even more bounce than the original. The *Firetron* was a fluorescent version of the ball.

Table tennis ball (Ping-Pong ball)

In its early days it was surrounded by wine and champagne. Later, it was at the center of a health and wellness program that might have helped fight drug addiction.

More recently, it has changed its size to make it more attractive on television. Sounds like the story arc for a Hollywood diva, but it's actually the history of the table tennis ball.

British Army officers were among the first to bring the popular Victorian game of lawn tennis indoors and onto a table in the 1880s. With no formal equipment on the market, these enterprising military personnel fashioned balls out of the rounded end of wine or champagne corks. Cigar box lids were used as paddles and books as a net.

With no standard rules or materials, the game was

haphazard. But it did draw the attention of sporting goods makers who believed a commercial version could be a moneymaker. In 1890, one entrepreneur named David Foster unveiled a set with strung racquets and a rubber ball wrapped in cloth. Prominent London sports equipment manufacturer John Jaques countered with a webbed cork ball and bats covered with a thin animal hide substance called vellum. He named his rendering *Gossima*. Neither game's sphere proved reliable: Foster's rubber ball bounced too much, while Jaques's didn't bound enough.

The answer to the perfect ball came from the same synthetic material that had revolutionized the billiard ball: celluloid (see page 28). These thin, hollow plastic balls were first produced in America. When a man named James Gibbs brought them back to England, the adroit Jaques pounced on them as the lynchpin for a new version of the game dubbed *Ping-Pong* after the sound the ball made off the paddles. Sold at London's famous Hamleys toy store, Ping-Pong sets became essential home entertainment for the wealthy in the first decade of the twentieth century. The initial enthusiasm sparked dances, biscuits, and even songs. "The Ballad of Ping-Pong," released in 1905 by well-known British poet Harry Graham, declared: *"Let the timorous turn to their tennis / Or the bowls to which bumpkins belong / But the thing for grown women and men is / The pastime of ping and of pong."*

By the mid-1920s, the more dignified term *table tennis* had formally replaced *Ping-Pong* as the official name of the game. The sport became particularly popular in Eastern Europe and Japan. Through those channels it ultimately spread to China, where the country's future supreme leader Mao Zedong became a fan. In 1949, following the Communist Party's rise to power, Mao opted to make table tennis a central national sport. There is disagreement over his motives. Some claim it was a move to galvanize the people, while others assert it was part of a health and wellness movement. A third explanation is that it was practiced as a form of drug rehabilitation. Opium use was rampant in China following World War II, and Mao believed that the concentration required to follow the little white Ping-Pong ball was impossible if under the influence of narcotics. The sport, in a sense, would force drug users to sharpen up. Whatever the case may be, in 1971 table tennis became an essential political and cultural bridge between the United States and China when a group of American players traveled to China in what was dubbed *Ping-Pong Diplomacy*.

The sport has endured, but the biggest issue has been making it more television friendly. With balls being hit at more than 100 miles per hour with incredible spins, table tennis organizers made a bold change in 2000, increasing the diameter of the golf ball–sized orb. The new ball is said to lower speed by some 8 percent and spin by as much as 13 percent, leading to longer, more pleasing rallies that are easier for couch potato viewers to follow.

STATS AND FACTS

Dimensions: 1.575 inches in diameter and 2.7 grams in weight. (The old ball was 0.079 inch smaller.)

Other Uses: The table tennis ball is versatile. Throw them in a hopper and use them for bingo games or lottery draws. During World War II specially treated balls were used by escaping POWs to light the way for planes. If you want to stay on a table, there's *Beer Pong*, a beloved college drinking game in which players try to knock the ball into cups of beer.

Language: Along with Ping-Pong, Gossima, and table tennis, a host of other names vied for the title of the sport in its early days. They included *whiff whaff, pom-pom, pim-pam, netto,* and *parlour tennis*.

Takraw (Raga)

For Americans, mentioning a rattan ball will likely conjure up images of Crate & Barrel catalogs or a home décor display at the mall. But in Southeast Asia, it is a

tool for an athletic game that's a cross between volleyball and soccer.

Though it might not come immediately to mind as a material for a sports ball, rattan, a durable and splinter-resistant type of palm, has served as the building block for spheres in such countries as Malaysia, Thailand, and the Philippines for centuries. The rattan orbs were at the center of a noncompetitive feet-only game dating back to the fifteenth century. The sphere was typically a hollow ball about the size of a small melon, and players stood in a circle attempting to keep the ball in the air. Depending on the country, it's had different names. In Malaysia and neighboring Brunei and Singapore, it's traditionally known as the *raga* ("rattan ball"), while in Thailand, the sphere is called the *takraw* ("woven ball").

As for who turned this community game without winners into a hot-blooded sport, not surprisingly, there is some competitive disagreement. In the nineteenth century, Thailand's Siam Sports Association printed rules for a competitive game using the rattan ball, while the Malaysians also lay claim to the sport's roots. This debate got particularly heated in the run-up to the 1965 Southeast Asia Peninsular Games. Malaysia was hosting the event and wanted to include the rattan kicking game on the program. Other countries liked the idea, but there was a problem. The Malaysians called the sport *sepak raga*, which means "kick rattan ball" in their native tongue. Representatives from Thailand and elsewhere believed that giving the game a Malaysian name didn't fully recognize the sport's roots elsewhere. After much debate, the parties compromised on *sepak takraw*, which combines the Malaysian word for "kick" (*sepak*) with the Thai term for "woven ball" (*takraw*).

With an accord—and a name—in place, the game flourished. Competitors typically rise above the sport's five-foot-one-inch-high net to kick the ball at speeds up to 90 miles per hour. This power has required some changes to the takraw. Despite its resiliency, the rattan ball would splinter or break apart after a really hard spike kick (it was also increasingly difficult to come by with overharvesting of the plant). The ball continues to be made in the centuries-old handwoven fashion and design, but synthetic fibers are now the norm.

Still, some disagreement remains. In 2007, the Malaysian sepak takraw team pulled out of the Southeast Asian Games because of the consistency of the ball. Thai organizers named a new takraw that had a rubber coating as the official ball for the event. The Malaysians claimed that the sphere was too hard and bounced too inconsistently. Rather than subject its players to the dangerous new orb, the team walked. The days of noncompetitive kicking around are undoubtedly over.

STATS AND FACTS

Dimensions: The men's ball is between 16.5 and 17.25 inches in circumference and weighs from 6 to 6.3 ounces. The women's ball is slightly larger (17 to 17.75 inches) and a bit lighter (5.3 to 5.4 ounces).

Language: A team, which is made up of three starters and one substitute, is called a *regu*. The player serving is known as the *tekong*.

Team handball

The original team handball wasn't just a sphere used to tally goals—it was a Nazi propaganda prop. In 1936, the fascist Germans hosted the Berlin Olympic Games and its leaders were given the option of adding one game. The Third Reich did not hesitate: It opted for an outdoor version of team handball called *field handball*. Played on a large field (using a soccer ball–sized sphere), this was essentially soccer played with hands. The Germans claimed it as a "native sport" and figured they could wield the bulky handball better than any opponent and score an easy gold medal. They were right. The Nazi team crushed the five other countries in the competition, including the United States 29–1.

World War II put an end to the German-embraced outdoor version of the game. But the sport resumed after the war primarily in a shrunken fashion. Scandinavians—who are no strangers to creating small, functional indoor options (see IKEA)—were instrumental in developing a gym version of team handball. Featuring a smaller ball (about the size of a large cantaloupe), this game has developed into a cross between soccer and basketball. While the object is still scoring goals in a soccer-like net (à la field handball), basketball components such as free throws and dribbling now exist. Compared to the field format, it also has fewer players (seven on a side as opposed to eleven for the outdoor variation); is contested on a court slightly bigger than a basketball court (in contrast to a sprawling field); and can be regularly enjoyed during the frigid, dark winter months. Proving that bigger is not always better, the little ball version returned to the Olympics in 1972 for the first time since the 1936 games and has remained a part of the games ever since.

Today, both synthetic and leather balls are used in international competitions. A former Danish soccer goalkeeper named Eigil Nielsen trailblazed the development of team handballs in the late 1940s and early 1950s. His company, Select Sport A/S, boasts that their hand-stitched balls are the best as a result of specially treated latex bladders, which retain shape well and allow for better dribbling. There might be something to the claim as Select does supply Olympic team handball competitions.

STATS AND FACTS

Dimensions: The men's ball is approximately 23 to 24 inches in circumference and weighs about 15 to 17 ounces (the women's ball is around 2 inches smaller and weighs some 3 ounces less).

Variations: *Beach handball* is similar to the indoor version but played under the sun on the sand. A smaller rubber ball is used. Created in 1970 by a Swiss biologist, *Tchoukball* is a game utilizing a sphere much like the team handball.

Language: A key to the sport is the *three-step/three-second rule*. A player can take only three steps or hold on to the ball for only three seconds before dribbling, passing, or shooting. The goalkeeper is exempt from this rule under certain circumstances.

Tennis ball

Considering some early tennis balls were created by novice Christian theologians to honor God, one wonders how a John McEnroe–style tirade would have gone over in

the primitive days of tennis. Probably pretty poorly, but on the plus side for someone like the brassy McEnroe, the Divine One apparently liked big balls.

In the fourteenth century, student priests in the French town of Nevers were responsible for producing tennis balls. They believed that the larger the ball they produced, the more it reflected on their piety and spiritual zeal. These religious apprentices were tasked with manufacturing duties for games played by choir members as part of Easter customs. Members of the church hierarchy ultimately put an end to the practice partially—one would hope—for ecumenical reasons (they saw this as misdirected religious excitement); they also did it for a practical purpose. While the game was being played with rules somewhat similar to modern tennis, players weren't using racquets yet and these bigger balls were requiring players to volley with two hands, which was a cumbersome task.

The church would slowly recede from the game, allowing members of Europe's upper class (who had almost a religious attraction for the game themselves) to develop the sport. This initial form of tennis was known as *jeu de paume* and was much different from today's game. Most notably, players smacked balls around with their hands. With the widespread introduction of racquets by the start of the 1500s, organizers of the sport were forced to also develop sturdier balls to handle the pounding. Alas, there was no ball springy enough at that point to take outdoors so the sport was primarily an indoor activity. Still, getting some bounce was a necessity even on the hard indoor floors, which left artisans scrambling for just the right materials.

Leather or sheepskin casings were typical, but finding the perfect stuffing was far more vexing. Just about everything was tried—dog hair, moss, and sawdust. (The latter concerned many because the fine wood pieces could lead to hand injuries when the ball inevitably split.) But of all the choices, the oddest must have been human hair. In England, where the game had taken hold with the aristocracy (a tennis court was built at the Hampton Court Palace in 1530), it was not uncommon for ball makers to head to the local barbershop to get some stuffing. Even Shakespeare made light of this peculiar practice in *Much Ado About Nothing*. When Don Pedro makes a playful comment about Benedick, he is told by Claudio that "the barber's man hath been seen with him, and the old ornament of his cheek hath already stuffed tennis-balls."

For European monarchs who loved the game, the by-product of hair styling wouldn't do. England's Henry VIII was said to have played with light balls featuring cork centers. In France, Louis XI was so annoyed with the choice of ball guts that he banned such substances as sand, ground chalk, lime, and metal shavings in 1480. Apparently hair was okay for others, but the king insisted on balls featuring quality hides filled with wool. At the dawn of the seventeenth century, ball makers had come to their senses and a core of tightly wound cloth surrounded by tape was the norm. By this point, white cloth, which could be inexpensively swapped out when worn, was replacing leather exteriors.

As much as European royals loved this indoor version of the sport, the distraction of revolutions in the 1700s stifled its growth. (It turned out that a good beheading was a much more popular spectator sport.) It sprang back to life in a new outdoor form in the nineteenth century thanks to the rubber ball. Europeans were aware of bouncy rubber spheres dating back to 1528 when conquistador Hernán Cortés brought back examples to Spain's King Charles V from the New World. But the ability to mass-produce a rubber orb was elusive until an American inventor named Charles Goodyear figured out how to vulcanize rubber in 1839. Although some had dabbled with the springy ball outdoors, the man who gets credit for popularizing and codifying outdoor tennis—or *lawn tennis* as it's formally known—was a dandy named Major Walter Clopton Wingfield.

Wingfield came from one of England's oldest families, dating its lineage to before the Norman Conquest. The grandson of a vicar, Wingfield was a social climber who married the daughter of his general while serving in India. Presumably, he believed that inventing a game for wealthy classes would further enhance his position in society. So in 1873, he went to work on a game he dubbed *sphairistike* (Greek for "the art of playing ball"). With a name like *sphairistike*, Wingfield was obviously not a marketing genius. Legend has it that he eventually took the advice of Prime Minister Arthur Balfour and went with the title *lawn tennis* instead. Still, the game did catch on quickly with the Prince of Wales and many royal families throughout Europe purchasing a set of balls, racquets, and a net.

Wingfield's first tennis package included gray rubber balls sourced from Germany, but with such high-class clientele, improvements were a must. To that end, white flannel covers for the rubber balls went into use in 1874, leading to better visibility and more consistent play. Top players considered the maintenance of these rubber orbs paramount. "Balls must be treated with some consideration; they must not be kept in cold damp cupboards, and if they are once touched by the frost, they are useless. As a rule, balls of a previous season are no good. The only balls now used are undersewn.... Uncovered balls are an abomination," wrote a seemingly edgy H.W.W. Wilberforce, a Wimbledon doubles champ in 1887.

Considering his concern about cold places, Wilberforce

probably approved of the change from cloth to snug wool, which occurred by the beginning of the twentieth century. (The wool cover would later be replaced by a blend of nylon, wool, and cotton.) The ball continued to get a makeover in the 1920s when elastic cement sealant replaced stitching. In a move that really rattled traditionalists, *optic yellow* began replacing white as the color of choice for balls in the early 1970s. This move was for commercial reasons: The dazzling yellow hue was easier to see on television. It took the venerable Wimbledon more than a decade to accept the luminescent balls for its tournament.

Creating the modern product is an exacting business. Engineers work to have just enough fuzz on the ball to allow racquet faces to get good friction, but not too much to slow the ball down aerodynamically. After the covering is attached to the rubber ball, it is steam-fluffed by industrial dryers in order to reach optimal fuzz. Once completed, balls are also checked for proper pressure, bounciness, and roundness (balls must meet a standard within five-thousandths of an inch for the U.S. Open). It's a type of exactness that even the most earnest monks would have been hard-pressed to achieve.

STATS AND FACTS

Dimensions: Balls must be between 2.5 and 2.625 inches in diameter and weigh 2 to 2.0625 ounces.

Strange But True: Tennis-loving royalty have not always been rewarded for their support of the game. Two French kings suffered tennis-related deaths. Louis X perished after contracting a severe chill following a tennis (*jeu de paume*) match, and Charles VIII died after striking his head on a low lintel over a stairway on his way to a court. James I, King of Scotland, was killed by conspirators on February 20, 1437, because, according to one account, just three days earlier he had blocked off what could have been an escape route. The reason for the closure: His tennis balls were getting stuck in the passage. Some also attribute the death of British King George II's son Frederick, Prince of Wales, to an injury sustained while playing tennis. "Poor Fred" was hit in the stomach by a ball and doctors thought his death three years later may have been caused by that blow. (Some claim he was actually hit with a cricket ball so the jury is still out on this one.)

Shakespeare and Tennis: Shakespeare references tennis in no less than six plays: *Hamlet*; *Henry IV, Part Two*; *Henry VIII*; *Much Ado About Nothing*; *Pericles*; and *Henry V*. The *Henry V* mention is probably the most famous. The British king is offended by the French dauphin's gift of tennis balls, which leads to the invasion of France and the Battle of Agincourt. (This supposed fact is almost certainly fictional.)

Language: Most agree that the term *tennis* comes from the French word *tenez*, which means "take this." It is thought that early players yelled out *"Tenez"* before hitting the ball. But author Julian Norridge points out in his book *Can We Have Our Balls Back, Please?* that the *Oxford English Dictionary* says that "no mention of this call has yet been found in French," suggesting the etymology of the word is still an open question.

Tetherball

Picture a group of New York's elite at a seaside estate all clamoring to play tetherball. If that isn't befuddling enough, imagine the Notre Dame football team sparking

a craze for the game, which involves whacking a ball attached to a rope around a pole, on the famed South Bend, Indiana, campus. Yes, there was a time when tetherball was actually cool.

Today, it's the domain of preteens or the eternally awkward (the 2004 comedy film *Napoleon Dynamite* provides all the necessary evidence), but in 1899, the *New York Times* decreed that tetherball was "making its way at the fashionable resorts and bids fair to check the growing popularity of the old favorite croquet, and also of tennis." Even as late as 1942, tetherball wasn't the playground game we're accustomed to. That year, a Fighting Irish halfback named John Peasenelli brought the game to Notre Dame. Teammate Fred "Dippy" Evans, who would go on to score the first touchdown in Cleveland Browns history, helped spread tetherball throughout the school.

How the game went from a popular adult activity to a kid's frivolity has mostly to do with the ball that swings from the rope attached to the tetherball pole. When the game was invented in the early 1880s, the dangling sphere was much smaller, generally the size of a tennis ball. The rubber sphere was initially put in a little netting at the bottom of an elastic cord and players would smack it with paddles or with their bare hand. In this format, it was heralded as a game of skill similar to lawn tennis but lacking the bother of having to chase after errant shots.

However, ball manufacturer W. J. Voit Rubber Corp. had other plans for tetherball. Always looking to expand its line of kid-friendly orbs—Voit was also instrumental in creating beach balls (see page 22) and red playground balls (see page 134)—the company introduced a volleyball-sized version of tetherball in 1948. This new easily whackable ball was made to take the pounding of the elementary school set. Constructed of a tough but smooth white waterproof rubber, the ball was washable for high visibility and was advertised as "easy on the hands." Other companies also came out with their versions of the tetherball. Most were rubber, though some tried selling leather versions. Voit's key to success was creating a recess at the top of the ball so that the hook used to connect the nylon rope to the ball wouldn't smack a player's hand on a bad hit.

The big ball version of the game grew quickly. According to *Popular Science* magazine, twelve times as many people were playing tetherball in 1954 as in 1948. Cryptically, the publication didn't give a starting number, but it's safe to say that the easy-to-install 10-foot poles were popping up in backyards and on school playgrounds throughout the United States. Over time, the game lost momentum. There were a few instances of tetherball-related deaths (the rope and ball can swing at an unforgiving speed, sadly strangling some younger players), and for whatever reason, the game hasn't enjoyed the type of organized competition among misty-eyed adults as other nostalgic kids' sports such as dodgeball and kickball.

Nevertheless, tetherball is a childhood touchstone for many. In 1997, newscaster Katie Couric told colleagues on a CNBC telecast that the greatest Christmas gift she ever received was a tetherball set. "I was awesome at tetherball," Couric gushed. "Even though I was short, I loved to jump and hit it really, really hard 'cause I wasn't aggressive as a young person at all."

STATS AND FACTS

Dimensions: 8.25 inches in diameter and weighs 13.25 ounces.

Ball Variations: Some companies offer extra-soft tetherballs created to provide a "no sting game." The original smaller tetherball still exists; it's now referred to as *paddle tetherball*.

Language: A *pole drop* occurs when both players commit a violation such as touching the rope or double hitting the ball. To restart play, each player puts one hand on the ball. They then release the sphere toward the pole; after it hits the pole, either player is allowed to smack the ball again.

Ulama ball

Sport's sexiest sphere may very well be the Mesoamerican ulama ball. It's an ancient soft rubber orb nearly as heavy as a medicine ball and about the size of a volleyball that requires the hip action of Elvis Presley. The reason: The ball is bounced in the air off the side of the midriff. Think volleyball for the hips. The object of the game, which is played between two teams, is to keep the ball aloft by sending it off the hip over a line to the opposing side. It's no wonder that when Christopher Columbus first arrived in Santo Domingo and saw a rubber ball bound with such spring, he thought it was the work of Satan.

The lusty hip movements are not lost on ulama players, and many terms used in the sport spring with sexual innuendo. (I'll leave it to the imagination as to what's said about foamy latex used in the ball-making process.) Competitors certainly need stamina to handle the ulama orb. Participants must build up calloused hips in order to endure the constant pounding of the heavy sphere, which has been known to fly through the air at speeds up to 30 miles per hour. Some ancient players even wore leather hip yolks to deal with this problem. Moreover, games can last for days thanks to complex rules that can send one team's point total down to zero on a single play.

Despite a history that dates back to at least 1000 BC, the game and its traditional ball are nearly extinct. Conquistadors banned the sport in the sixteenth century, seeing it as an anti-Christian activity. In Mexico, where ulama still exists, there are only about 100 players, estimates James Brady, an ulama expert and professor at California State University–Los Angeles. One of the key factors for its continued demise is the inability to produce enough balls. In the regions where the sport is played, rubber trees are either no longer abundant or exist in areas controlled by the drug lords.

Thousands of years before the Western world figured out how to shape rubber, ulama balls were crafted through a natural vulcanization process. Supporters of the game have attempted to come up with a synthetic alternative, but have struggled to produce a ball with the same qualities of hardness or softness and the exact bounce needed for the sport. For the sexiest ball, you just can't fake it.

STATS AND FACTS

Dimensions: The ball sizes varied greatly, but typically were about 8 inches in diameter and could weigh up to 9 pounds.

Bettor's Game: One reason Spanish explorers were likely turned off by ulama was all the serious gambling that swirled around the game. One story tells of a man who wagered his daughter into slavery on an ulama contest. Some versions of the game also reportedly included human sacrifice.

Language: The Aztecs called a rubber ball an *olli* (from *ollin*, their word for "motion"). The Spanish based the sport's name *ollama* or *ulama* on that term.

Volleyball

When William G. Morgan successfully invented volleyball in Holyoke, Massachusetts, in 1895, he must have invoked the real estate mantra "location, location, location."

MASSACHUSETTS

HOLYOKE

CHICOPEE

Sure, by all accounts, Holyoke is a wonderfully bucolic hamlet, but more important, its spot on the map paved the way for a ball that could really keep his new sport aloft.

Not long after becoming the director of the YMCA in Holyoke, Morgan decided he wanted to offer a new sport to businessmen who were coming to the gym. Taking some inspiration from tennis, he figured a game in which players had to keep the ball in the air might do the trick (apparently, basketball was too rowdy for Morgan's gentle patrons). He tried volleying a basketball back and forth with the local fireman, but found that the tough leather sphere hurt his wrists. Playing with just the bladder was more pleasing, but the light ball was a bit difficult to control.

Where does one go when he needs to create an entirely new ball for a recently invented sport? In the case of Morgan, he just had to take a brisk walk about 5 miles downstream to the town of Chicopee. Morgan had the good fortune of being located right next door to A. G. Spalding and Brothers, the country's preeminent sporting goods manufacturer. In these pre-FedEx days, Morgan put together some specifications and was able to get a prototype in reasonable time. Spalding's first effort used a supple calfskin cover that didn't hold up well, but a second effort, using lighter but more durable leather similar to the basketball, was just right.

Over the years many rules in volleyball have changed. For example, the height of the net has increased by more than a foot and "dribbling" the ball (upward on one's hands rather than on the ground like basketball) was allowed and then discarded. But with the exception of a brief unsuccessful size increase at the start of the twentieth century, the dimensions of the volleyball have remained practically constant since Morgan's original design. That doesn't mean the sphere has not been updated dramatically. The essence of the volleyball is very much in details.

If you think a volleyball floats more than other spheres, there's a reason for that. Most volleyballs in the United States are constructed with three main pieces: a bladder and a cotton or nylon cloth layer glued to outer leather panels. Unlike a basketball, the volleyball's bladder is not attached to the outer casing, allowing a pocket of air to provide a little additional softness to the ball. (This style is called "loose bladder construction"—insert your own joke here.) As was the case with Morgan, location seems to be everything when it comes to this design. While Americans tend to like the air pocket, players elsewhere in the world typically opt for a connected bladder, which leads to a harder, faster ball.

STATS AND FACTS

Dimensions: The ball must be between 25.5 and 26.5 inches in circumference and weigh 9 to 10 ounces.

Updated Look: In 2007, volleyball's international federation introduced a new ball. Changes included an eight-panel flower petal design, dimples to help the ball move more accurately in the air, and wait for it . . . *color*! Indoor volleyballs were white across the board until this move, which decreed a blue and yellow combo for better visibility. Since then other color schemes have popped up as well.

Variation: Beach volleyball hit the sands of California in the 1920s. To overcome those nice ocean breezes, players use a slightly bigger ball than the indoor version in order to cut through the wind.

Language: Morgan's initial name for his game was *mintonette*. Where he got that term from is unclear. Some scholars say it comes from an Indian game *minton*, which featured players keeping a smaller ball in the air with rackets. The *ette* suffix was added to indicate that Morgan's new game was "similar to" or "like" that game. Another explanation is that the game was like badminton (no explanation why he didn't just go all the way and call it *goodminton*). Thankfully, Morgan took the advice of a friend and changed the name of the game to *volleyball*.

Water polo ball

In the early days of water polo, the ball was practically incidental to the game. Invented in Great Britain during the 1860s, the sport was original known as *aquatic football* and it was more of a scrum than anything. Ominous-sounding maneuvers such as *the back stranglehold* or the *jujitsu toe hold* were all part of trying to prevent opponents from physically crossing a goal line (à la rugby).

At first, the ball was made of dense India rubber, and some players would stuff it in their swimsuit, dive down underwater, and try to evade the various popular wrestling moves en route to the goal. Sensing a change was necessary—if for no other reason than to avoid all-out water warfare—organizers replaced the easily hidden solid sphere with a white inflatable rubber ball (or in some parts of the world a leather sphere) about the size of a soccer ball. But even that transformation had a caveat in the United States. The balls were only inflated seven-eighths full. That meant players could still easily grab the orb and pile-drive their way across the pool.

In 1902, rules in America changed to require a fully inflated ball. The warriors of the old game were not thrilled, saying the inability to easily carry the pumped-up ball led to "constant fumbling [and] made the game a farce," the *New York Times* reported. Players adjusted, but the ball still needed fine-tuning. A Southern California water polo coach named Jimmy Smith was annoyed at how leather-covered balls commonly being used in international play were becoming waterlogged. After the ball performed like a lead weight at the 1936 Olympic Games, Smith took matters into his own hands.

He contacted Voit, a successful inflatable ball manufacturer, and they set to work on a better ball. What they came up with was a rubber-covered sphere that had grip but didn't get super-soaked. The original was red but in the late 1940s it was changed to its iconic *optic yellow* color. One myth claims the shift occurred because balls were being produced with the same rubber fabric used to make the brightly hued World War II "Mae West" life jackets. While that story is almost certainly fictional, the new color offered excellent visibility, and college and high school federations went so far as to explicitly require every game ball to be yellow.

Though improvements have continued through the years—most notably, a version that skipped more easily on the water became the norm in the 1980s—the ball always remained yellow with black seams. Finally in 2006, the sport's various governing bodies agreed to multicolored designs. Proving there is still fight in water polo, some schools were weary of the new look. The reason: They refused to use balls featuring the color scheme of their biggest rivals.

STATS AND FACTS

Dimensions: Sizes range from 28 inches (for men) to 26 inches (for women) in circumference. Weights vary from 14 to 16 ounces.

Language: Hard play still exists in water polo. *Brutality* is a term for a foul that inflicts intentional bodily harm on an opponent.

Wiffle Ball

In 1953, David Nelson Mullany was a former college and semipro baseball player in an industrial corner of Connecticut looking for a break. Unemployed, Mullany watched as his thirteen-year-old son played a modified version of baseball using a broomstick and a plastic golf ball. When his son started complaining that trying to throw a curveball with the little sphere was hurting his arm, Mullany went to work. He cut holes in a spherical-shaped plastic perfume package. It took more than a dozen tries, but finally, voilà, he had a softer-than-hard-ball plastic sphere. With the holes, the ball curved easily, making it a challenge for batters to hit—and easier on his boy's arm.

His son suggested calling it a whiffle ball (named after the slang for a batter swinging and missing—a "whiff").

Still, ever concerned about his dad's financial situation, David's son advised spelling the name without the *h*. "If we ever have to make a sign for over the door," the boy

explained, "that's one less letter we'll have to pay for." An entrepreneur at heart, the elder Mullany mortgaged his home to start selling the new product. He bought an injection molding machine and leased space at a nearby factory. His first sale: a local restaurant, which agreed to sell the Wiffle Ball in its front window at 49 cents a ball.

Patented in 1957, the Wiffle Ball design featured eighteen slotted holes on one side of the ball and solid plastic on the other. (The current design has eight longer holes.) A variety of alternatives have come to the market since Mullany's innovation. Some have holes throughout the ball, while others have holes just in the middle. Each requires different grips to cause movement in various directions. The result of a properly thrown Wiffle pitch can be movement either up, down, left, or right as much as 4 feet—about double the distance of a Major League curveball. The orb can also be thrown at a blistering pace from short distances. One radar gun had a Wiffle Ball clocked at 75 miles per hour from a pitcher's rubber 42 feet from home plate. From a Major League mound at 60 feet, 6 inches, that speed would translate into a 105-mile-per-hour fastball.

The company has experimented with Wiffle golf balls, basketballs, and footballs, but none has been a money spinner. Still, today, Wiffle Ball Inc., of Shelton, Connecticut, remains a successful family-owned business thanks to its original design.

STATS AND FACTS

Dimensions: The original has a 9-inch circumference and weighs 1.6 ounces.

Used With: The most popular item to hit a Wiffle Ball with is a Wiffle Bat. The original was 31 inches long and possessed an ultra-skinny 1.125-inch-diameter barrel. Today, a 32-inch version is sold; there are also aluminum variations now on the market.

Advertising: The Wiffle Ball used to rely heavily on Major League Baseball players to sell the orb. Early endorsers included future Hall of Famers Whitey Ford and Ted Williams, but over time, the Mullany family decided that the value of the famous pitchmen did not exceed the cost.

Language: A practitioner of the game of Wiffle Ball is called a *Wiffler*.

Zorb Globe

When Dwane van der Sluis and Andrew Akers invented a ball that allowed them to perform a divine feat and then realized that it wasn't the sphere's coolest trick, they

knew they'd come up with something pretty impressive. The New Zealand natives had been obsessed with figuring out a way to walk on water. In 1994, they set up shop in Akers's garage and came up with the *Zorb Globe*, a huge ball that you can climb into and looks like a human hamster plaything.

Thrilled, they took it down to the ocean but quickly found that walking on water wasn't all it was cracked up to be. It was tiring and they were actually blown out to sea on a few occasions. They then made a revelatory discovery: Tumbling down hills inside a Zorb Globe—an act called *zorbing*—was just the type of adrenaline-pumping fun that people will pay money to enjoy. To paraphrase the film *Caddyshack*, you can literally be the ball.

Actually, the company offers two different balls. There is the *Harness Globe*, in which you are strapped into the center of the ball and roll down the hill. (Zorbing has its own courses located throughout the world.) The alternative experience is the *Hydro Globe*. Forget the harness and add about 5 gallons of water. As the ball tumbles down the hill, riders—or *zorbonauts*, as the inventors call them—slip and slide in the H_2O. This experience has been likened to being a pair of socks in a washing machine.

Both globes are essentially constructed the same way. There are actually two transparent, inflatable plastic balls that make up the Zorb Globe. A nearly 10-foot-in-diameter outer ball is connected to an interior ball (about 6 feet in diameter) by a myriad of nylon ties. Air is pumped into the space between the two balls to create cushioning for the riders, who enter through a 2-foot-wide hole that also ensures oxygen gets to the zorbonauts once they climb inside. Up to three people can slosh around in the Hydro Globe, while the nonwater version is a solo affair.

Zorbing downhill may beat walking on water, but there are limitations. The ball cannot roll down a hill at greater than a 20-degree angle. "Any steeper and it starts bouncing and bouncing and bouncing," confided Andrew Akers ominously in a 1999 *Sports Illustrated* article. While courses vary, the typical ride goes roughly 500 to 700 feet and lasts at least 40 seconds. It sounds like a stomach-churning experience, but the supersize of the ball means that it will only make a single rotation for every 30 feet it rolls, so you're not spinning like a baseball in flight. Most zorbonauts reach speeds of 20 miles per hour. The record for longest roll is nearly 1,872 feet; the fastest globe clocked in at 32 miles per hour.

Along with the typical extreme sport thrill seekers, an eclectic group has been drawn to the Zorb Globe. Musician Peter Gabriel used one on his 2003 Growing Live Tour, while television shows such as *The Amazing Race*, *Road Rules*, and *Top Gear* have featured the globe on their programs. Sea World requested a globe for a show it once did, and even Jet Propulsion Laboratories asked for the big ball in conjunction with Mars landing research it was doing for NASA.

Still, the inventors have been somewhat discerning when it comes to sharing their creation. In 2002, the alternative rock band Flaming Lips wanted to use a globe. After listening to the group's album *Yoshimi Battles the Pink Robots*, co-inventor Akers refused to provide one, according to the inventors' website. We can only assume he didn't approve of the music. The band had to settle for constructing their own version in order to perform a crowd surfing feat in which the audience holds up the ball. Alas, no word on whether the band members can walk on water in their big ball.

STATS AND FACTS

Dimensions: The ball is approximately 10 feet in diameter (though it can range up to 12 feet) and weighs between 198 and 220 pounds.

Fallout: The original inventors are no longer involved with the company that produces the Zorb Globe. Van der Sluis left the organization to pursue other interests in 1996, while Akers departed from the business in 2006 because he was "frustrated by an increasingly corporate culture imposed by [the] new regime controlling the company," according to his website.

International Appeal: There are zorbing sites throughout the world. The original location is on the North Island of New Zealand in Rotorua, while zorbing can be enjoyed in Pigeon Forge, Tennessee, in the United States. Other manufacturers have attempted to get into the inflatable riding ball business, but makers of the Zorb Globe are quick to point to their strict safety measures and attention to manufacturing detail as a competitive advantage.

Language: The world *Zorb* reportedly comes from the word *orb* with a *Z* tacked in front in honor of the Kiwi inventors' native land.

X-TRA BALLS

In case you haven't fully gotten your ball fix, here are a few additional ball sports (and their balls) that didn't quite make the cut for a full entry:

1. *Doonee*: Invented in Argentina in the 1970s, this sport looks a bit like a catch-and-throw version of volleyball—although two high nets are used. It features a larger-than-basketball-sized hollow ball called the *COR* that resembles a series of balloon animals tied together to make a globe. (You can find it on YouTube.)
2. *Fistball*: The name of this game is a bit unfortunate. In Germany, where the sport is mainly played, it's called *Faustball*, which sounds a lot better. The sport uses a sphere called the *Drohnn ball*, which looks and plays somewhat like a volleyball. That said, the ball has a completely smooth waxed leather exterior

and different interior construction than its volleying cousin. (A *Prellball* is a similar sphere used for another volleyball-esque German game.)

3. *Foosball (table football):* Who would have thought that the stewards of everybody's favorite 2 a.m. beer-soaked pastime would need a different ball depending on the occasion? A recreational foosball is smooth and 1.3 inches in diameter, but a competition-grade version is larger and can feature a rough surface for better ball control.

4. *Korfball:* A Dutch sport that bears a strong resemblance to basketball without backboards, korfball uses a sphere that is utilized like a basketball, but according to one *Los Angeles Times* journalist in 1979, "looks suspiciously like a soccer ball with 'Official Korfball' stamped on it."

5. *Pato:* The longtime national sport of Argentina, *pato* (Spanish for "duck") is named after the game's original ball. In the seventeenth century, players on horseback would try to scoop up a live duck in a basket or leather pouch and then attempt to throw the bird into a raised net that looks like a giant version of those used to catch butterflies. Today, a ball fitted with six leather handles has mercifully replaced the packed-up duck.

6. *Pickleball:* A paddle game invented in Seattle, Washington, Pickleball uses a hollow plastic sphere that is quite similar to the Wiffle Ball.

7. *Skee-ball:* An arcade staple, Skee-ball appears to use baseball-sized wooden balls that are rolled toward holes with differing point totals.

8. *Street hockey (Roller hockey):* This sport was probably informally played for decades before Raymond Leclerc started selling specifically designed street hockey balls in the early 1970s. Through his company, Mylec Sports, Leclerc, a Canadian who had worked in the toy industry, manufactures street balls with little bounce, making them perfect for the street. Many other companies have followed.

ACKNOWLEDGMENTS

Thanks must first go out to my illustrator, Emily Stackhouse. It's an honor to have your work alongside my writing. Speaking of the writing, much appreciation goes to Jennifer and Dan for both hanging with me through this process and offering essential feedback about what I put on the page.

I interviewed numerous people for this book, but there was a group who were particularly helpful in providing information and insight: Bob Alman (croquet ball), James Brady (ulama ball), Harko Brown (ki), Lauren Harrington (team handball), Andy Havill (Zorb Globe), Antti Kallio (pallo), Mike May (sporting goods industry), Richard McCoy (volleyball, water polo ball, red playground ball), Urvasi Naidoo (netball), Leo Nikora (croquet ball), Vern Roberts (handball), Ian Savage (netball), Marc Schoenberg (pinball), Magnus Sköld (bandy ball), and Christopher Wolf (pinball).

Finally, tremendous gratitude goes out to Maria Gagliano at Perigee and Danielle Svetcov (my fantastic friend and book agent). Without your interest and willingness to move forward, this project never would have happened.

NOTES

For clarity and brevity, some quotes in this book do not have explicit references to their sources in the body of the work. Below is a rundown of where those quotes came from.

Introduction

xi "Y'didn't play with a ball today . . . so that's what I bleddy scored with!" Frank Keating, "The Ball's the Thing," *Spectator (UK)*, January 21, 2006, 71.

xiii "[g]ames played with the ball . . . stamp no character on the mind." David Block, *Baseball Before We Knew It: A Search for the Roots of the Game* (Lincoln: University of Nebraska Press, 2006), 271.

xiii "the [b]all must be some . . . enemy of the human race." Jerome K. Jerome, "Idle Thoughts," *N.C. Herald and S.C. & C. Gazette*, August 4, 1905, 274–75.

Baseball

15 "dazzling whiteness." Peter Morris, *A Game of Inches: The Game on the Field* (Chicago: Ivan R. Dee, 2006), 406.

Basketball

19 "The hardest . . . to hold its shape." Jackie MacMullan, "It's a Love Affair: 100 Years of Basketball," *Boston Globe*, December 13, 1991, 98.

Croquet balls

44 "He could have . . . could never bear." Mike Orgill and David Drazin, "Who *Really* Won the Election of 1879?" *Croquet World Online Magazine*, November 2, 2008, www .croquetworld.com/News/election.asp.

45 "Paint them of as many . . . the pleasanter the play." Capt. Mayne Reid, *Croquet*, 1864, Chapter 3, www.oxfordcroquet .com/history/1864/chapter_3.asp.

Footbag (Hacky Sack)

53 "[Marshall's] death was devastating . . . Mike and I had started." Tim Walsh, *Wham-O Super-Book: Celebrating 60 Years Inside the Fun Factory* (San Francisco: Chronicle Books, 2008), 45.

Football

57 "looks like a Long Island frankfurter." Mal Florence, "Vince Lombardi Undecided About Coaching Future," *Los Angeles Times*, January 13, 1968, A2.

Golf ball

65 "Without question the most . . . of the wound ball." Larry Dennis and Udo Machat, *The Golf Ball Book* (Oakland, Calif.: Sports Images, 2000), 45.

Jai alai pelota

71 "the most lethal ball used in sports." Freida Ratliff Frisaro, "'Pelota' Maker Uses Off-Court Jai-Alai Skills," *Ocala (FL) Star Banner,* June 25, 1987, 1B.

Koosh Ball

77 "a cross between Jell-O and a porcupine." Sally Vallongo, "The Right Toy for the Times," *Toledo Blade,* April 28, 1989, 12.

77 "I intuitively knew...do the trick." Elizabeth A. Brown, "Colorful Koosh Balls Catch On," *Christian Science Monitor,* July 25, 1989, 14.

79 "a process of surveys and logic," "Little Brainstorms, Big Bucks," *People,* August 3, 1998, www.people.com/people/archive/article/0,20125913,00.html.

Lacrosse ball

81 "a pretty Canadian...any uncultivated squaw." W. G. Beers, *Lacrosse: The National Game of Canada* (Montreal: Dawson Brothers, 1869), 33.

Lawn bowling balls

85 "A Bowling-green...the last ten for one." Joseph Strutt, *The Sports and Pastimes of the People of England* (London: Methuen & Co., 1801), 219.

Marbles

90 "in the presence...play marbles." "Balls and Marbles Prohibited," *New York Times,* October 6, 1882.

90 "positively immoral...all its tendencies." "Playing Marbles for Keeps," *New York Times,* May 10, 1888.

91 "You haven't any business to play . . . You are on the road to perdition." "Boys Arrested for Playing Marbles," *New York Times*, November 20, 1894.

Presidential balls

94 "I would like to deny . . . an elk and a moose." Eric Zweig, *Par for the Course: Golf's Best Quotes and Quips* (Richmond Hill, Ont.: Firefly Books, 2007), 126.

94 "a health-inspiring . . . otherwise fatigued mind." "Game Room," The White House Museum, www.whitehouse museum.org/floor3/game-room.htm.

Mari

96 "face powder." Bertha Clarke, "Elegant Sport in Japan. Quaint Football Game." *Sydney Morning Herald*, January 16, 1937.

97 "An ideal flick of the ball . . . should not be too low or too high." Akino Yoshihara (*Daily Yomiuri*), "Alive and Kicking: Group Seeks to Preserve Ancient Ball Game," *Asia Africa Intelligence Wire*, July 2, 2003.

Meditation balls

102 "Troy can afford . . . than I can." "It Pays to Be Cowboy Lineman," *Reading (PA) Eagle*, January 28, 1994, C2.

Nerf ball

106 "Nerf started as . . . turned into an umbrella word." Tim Walsh, *Timeless Toys: Classic Toys and the Playmakers Who Created Them* (Kansas City, Mo.: Andrews McMeel Publishing, 2004), 220.

Paintballs

110 "temperamental." Charles Gaines, "Who Thought This Was a Good Idea?" *Sports Illustrated*, December 6, 2004, http://sportsillustrated.cnn.com/vault/article/magazine/MAG1114400/1/index.htm.

Pallo

114 "was invented by Lauri [Pihkala] . . . described baseball to him when his battery was dead." Red Smith, "Wounded in Helsinki," *Baseball Digest*, October 1952, 23.

Pétanque boules

116 "At one point in the '80s . . . was destructive to both companies." "Nuptials End 40-Year Petanque Rivalry," *Montreal (Quebec) Gazette*, August 2, 1995, E1.

Pinball

121 "I saw people . . . thought to myself, 'That's perfect.'" Alan Citron, "The Rise and Fall of Pinball," *Pittsburgh Press*, December 14, 1982, B1.

Pink ball (Spaldeen, Pennsy Pinky)

123 "Because you'd lose the ball . . . You [had] to hit for location." Joan Walsh, "Inside Baseball: Willie Mays Talks About Stickball in Harlem, Today's Best Players and His Ban from the Game," *Salon*, July 13, 1999, www.salon.com/people/feature/1999/07/13/mays_interview.

Racquetball

132 "fanny," "When you hit the ball . . . a very satisfying noise," and "I'm just proud . . . played around the world." Frank

Litsky, "Joseph Sobek, the Inventor of Racquetball, Dies at 79," *New York Times*, March 31, 1998.

Roulette ball

139 "you cannot beat...money from it." M. P. Singh, *Quote Unquote (A Handbook of Quotations)* (New Delhi: Lotus Press, 2006), 147.

Rugby ball

142 "a wonder of...match balls up tight." "The Ball," Rugby Football History, www.rugbyfootballhistory.com/ball.htm.

Shot put

145 "casting of the stone." W. H. Grenfell, "Oxford v. Yale," *Fortnightly*, volume 62 (1894), 368.

146 "You've got to be...I'm in a different world." "Frenzied Record Breaker," *Life*, June 22, 1953, 86.

Sliotar

150 "We live in the real world...has migrated abroad." Michael Clifford and John Downs, "Foreign Sliotars Used in GAA Games," *Sunday Tribune (Ireland)*, September 7, 2008, N06.

Space Hopper

161 "It does take...your legs work at it." "People," *Sports Illustrated*, January 29, 1968, http://sportsillustrated.cnn.com/vault/article/magazine/MAG1148004/index.htm.

Squash ball

165 "the most vexatious issue," and "gave the walls a pleasant pink hue." James Zug, *Squash: A History of the Game* (New York: Simon & Schuster, 2003), 35 and 37.

Stress ball

167 "Maybe it'll make people ... couple of years longer." "Bounce Back from Worry with Stress Ball," *Boca Raton News* (*USA Weekend* insert), September 25, 1988, 22.

SuperBall

171 "It was a name ... networks picked up on it." Craig Davis, "Ultimate Game Wasn't Always Super," *Fort Lauderdale Sun-Sentinel*, January 17, 1989, 1A.

Table tennis ball

175 "Let the timorous ... of ping and of pong." Henry Graham, "The Ballad of Ping-Pong," *Century Illustrated Monthly Magazine*, volume 69 (1905), 863.

Tennis ball

185 "Balls must be treated ... are an abomination." H.W.W. Wilberforce, *Lawn Tennis* (London: George Bell & Sons, 1908), 17.

Tetherball

190 "I was awesome ... as a young person at all." CNBC News Transcripts, December 27, 1997, 10:30 a.m.

Wiffle Ball

199 "If we ever have to ... we'll have to pay for." Lee Green, "The Wiffle Effect: Wiffle Ball Goes Big Time—Well, Not So Big," *Atlantic Monthly*, June 2002, 88.

SOURCES AND FURTHER READING

This book is the product of a variety of sources. Interviews, magazine and newspaper articles, and books were the primary tools. For the most part, each ball required a different avenue of inquiry. As hard as I tried, I couldn't find a book that talked about *both* the ki and the Koosh Ball. Still, there have been a number of works that predate my effort that cover a selection of different balls—either directly or in passing. If you're interested, check out:

Ball, Bat and Bishop: The Origin of Ball Games (1947) by Robert W. Henderson

Balls! (2006) and *Balls! Round 2* (2008) by Michael J. Ross

The Big Book of Rules (2005) by Stephanie Spadaccini

Can We Have Our Balls Back, Please? How the British Invented Sport (and Then Almost Forgot How to Play It) (2008) by Julian Norridge

Games for the Playground, Home, School and Gymnasium (1909) by Jessie H. Bancroft

A Load of Old Balls (2005) by Simon Inglis

The Playmakers: Amazing Origins of Timeless Toys (2004) and *Whamo-O Super-Book: Celebrating 60 Years Inside the Fun Factory* (2008) by Tim Walsh

Sports and Games of the 18th and 19th Centuries (2003) by Robert Crego

While there wouldn't be enough space to mention every ball-specific volume that helped inform my work, here's a selection of some particularly useful and/or interesting ones:

Australian Rules football—*A Game of Our Own: The Origins of Australian Football* (2003) by Geoffrey Blainey

Ba'—*Uppies and Downies: The Extraordinary Football Games of Britain* (2008) by Hugh Hornby

Baseball—*A Game of Inches: The Game on the Field* (2006) by Peter Morris

Billiards—*Ivory's Ghosts: The White Gold of History and the Fate of Elephants* by John Frederick Walker (2009)

Croquet—*Croquet* (1864) by Captain Mayne Reid

Football—*Football* (1896) by Walter Camp and Lorin F. Deland

Gaelic football—*The History of Gaelic Football* (2009) by Eoghan Corry

Golf—*The Golf Ball Book* (2000) by Larry Dennis and Udo Machat

Lacrosse—*Lacrosse: Technique and Tradition* (2006) by David G. Pietramala, Neil A. Grauer, and Bob Scott

Polo—*The Evolution of Polo* (2009) by Horace A. Laffaye

Roulette—*Get the Edge at Roulette* (2001) by Christopher Pawlicki

Softball—*The Worth Book of Softball: A Celebration of America's True National Pastime* (1994) by Paul Dickson

Squash—*Squash: A History of the Game* (2003) by James Zug

Tennis—*Lawn Tennis* (1890) by C. G. Heathcote

Volleyball—*The Untold Story of William G. Morgan: Inventor of Volleyball* (2007) by Joel B. Dearing

ABOUT THE AUTHOR

Jennifer Riley Chetwynd

Josh Chetwynd is an award-winning journalist who has worked as a staff reporter for such publications as *USA Today* and *U.S. News & World Report*. When it comes to sports balls, his longest-lasting relationship has been with the baseball. He previously played at the college level at Northwestern University and professionally in both the United States and Europe. He's also broadcasted Major League Baseball games in Great Britain on BBC Radio and Channel 5, a national television network. That focus has not diminished his enthusiasm for other spherical projectiles and playthings. He has either owned or enjoyed more than forty of the balls in this book.